❋ LEADSOLOGY:®

Marketing
The Invisible

A proven model for generating a weekly flow of inquiries
from qualified prospects who want to work with you.

TOM
POLAND

Internationally Acclaimed
Inbound Lead Generation Specialist

'THE DIRECTOR'S CUT'

Here's the authors pick of the freshest and more powerful parts of this book.

- ✓ **WHY MARKETING THE INVISIBLE** is more like proposing marriage than selling a car.
- ✓ **WHY YOU SHOULD AVOID** these Ten commonly taught marketing methods.
- ✓ **THE TITANIUM TRIANGLE**: how to stimulate a weekly flow of inbound, new client inquiries
- ✓ **THE FOUR LEVELS OF PSYCHOLOGICAL ALLURE**: how to ethically create a magnetic attraction that is all but irresistible for ideal clients.
- ✓ **THE LEADSOLOGY® PERSUASION SEQUENCE**: a ten-part formula to embed into presentations, publications, and pitches that will dramatically improve response rates.
- ✓ **THE SEW SEGMENTATION FORMULA**: a simple formula that increases new client inquiries more than five-fold (literally).
- ✓ **THE FOUR VALIDATIONS**: what your ideal clients need to hear to confirm that investing with you is the right thing to do.
- ✓ **THE ORCHESTRA CONDUCTOR**: how to free up your time and scale your marketing results through a simple three-step process of segmentation, automation, and outsourcing.

FREE MARKETING RESOURCES

MARKETING IS LIKE life, in that it is a journey, not a destination. In addition to devouring this book, I recommend that you commit to furthering your lead-generation journey by…

ENROLLING in our free Five-Day Lead Generation Challenge at **www.fivehourchallenge.com**, which is by far our most popular zero-cost offering.

BOOK a time for us to talk embedding lead generation systems into your business by going to:
 www.bookachatwithtom.com

JOINING our Facebook group at:
www.facebook.com/groups/leadsology/ and gaining invitations to exclusive events such as my internationally acclaimed Lead Generation Boot Camp (free), as well as other online training events plus recommended resources, tips, and insights.

SUBSCRIBING to my Marketing The Invisible VLOGcast at **www.leadsology.guru/podcast** where I interview respected colleagues and contemporaries and ask them seven questions in just seven minutes.

VISITING **www.leadsology.guru/the-model/** and download the full interactive ten-part Leadsology® Model that reveals each step of the process for generating a steady flow of new client inquiries.

TAKING the Leadsology® Diagnostic challenge at:
www.leadsology.guru/diagnostic/ and receiving a fully

customized report identifying the exact items that your business needs to create a weekly flow of high-quality, inbound, new client inquiries.

Connecting with me on LinkedIn at: **https://au.linkedin.com/in/tompoland/** — another way of staying up-to-date on the latest developments here at Leadsology®.

Interview me www.leadsology.guru/podcastguest/

Invite me to speak at your conference by emailing me directly at **tom@leadsology.guru**

Follow me on Twitter: www.twitter.com/tompoland

DEDICATION

This book is dedicated to Paramahansa Yogananda, my spiritual guide.

Thank you for your wisdom, joy, and compassion.

And thank you especially for your whispers.

PRAISE FOR TOM POLAND'S PREVIOUS LEADSOLOGY®: BOOK: *THE SCIENCE OF BEING IN DEMAND*

THIS BOOK WILL BE IN DEMAND TOO

A terrific book. With trademark clarity and honesty, Tom Poland shows how trainers, consultants, and other advisers can generate a reliable flow of high quality leads. It's a really excellent method, and presented with verve and wit.

Richard Koch, Author of *The 80/20 Principle*, which sold over one million copies

ONE OF THE BEST BOOKS ON MARKETING EVER WRITTEN

Tom Poland is not only an expert marketer but a master teacher. Step- by-step instructions are easy to follow and you can build a complete marketing system without needing to be a genius. More practical and actionable than the 4-year marketing degree I completed.

Richard Petrie, Speed Marketing

EASILY ONE OF THE MOST VALUABLE BUSINESS BOOKS I'VE READ

By this point, I must have read over 400 books on marketing, sales and business and I can honestly say I found this one of the most valuable. So much useful stuff in Tom's book; it's accessible and Tom is a charming, down-to-earth guide, but the methodology is rigorous too. It's never dumbed down or over-simplified, because there is a lot to the Leadsology® model.

Tom's model gives you not only a ton of useful ideas, but the overarching framework you need to fit them together. It's a complete system, and it gives you clarity.

Rob Tyson, The Tyson Report

FABULOUS!

Leadsology® gives you the science behind figuring out EXACTLY how to create demand and generate a flow of high quality leads. Buy this book and put the formula to work in your business - the results speak for themselves.

**Dr Ivan Misner, Founder Business Network International (BNI)
and New York Times best-selling author**

A BOOK DEFINITELY WORTH BUYING

Business books that you don't want to put down are very rare, but Tom Poland's "Leadsology®" is one of them. Tom Poland goes right to the heart of lead generation in this wonderful book, which is full of real world wisdom.

As the author of 47 books, I hate having to say that I wish I had written this one! It has certainly given me loads of ideas for improving my next book.

If I ever get chance, I will invite Tom Poland to address my MBA students in one of the world's top Business Schools. They really need to know and understand material like this.

**Professor Malcolm McDonald MA(Oxon) MSc PhD DLitt DSc,
Emeritus Professor, Cranfield University School of Management,
Author of *Marketing Plans* which sold over 500,000 copies**

A MUST-READ BOOK

Brilliant! Leadsology® lays out a step-by-step process for advisors who want to create a cut-through marketing message and get the message out to the marketplace so that inbound new client inquiries flow in like turning on a tap.

In particular, I recommend searching the book for "The Waterfall," "The Dinner Party Question," and "The Value Slider," which are all original and brilliant concepts that the author has introduced. As a successful consultant for over a decade, I recognize marketing gold when I see it.

Ari Galper, Author of *Unlock The Game*

DON'T THINK ABOUT IT, GRAB THIS BOOK NOW AND BREAK DOWN THE BARRIERS HOLDING YOUR BUSINESS BACK!

Tom Poland's book is a great resource that lays out common entrepre-

neur pitfalls for coaches, consultants, advisors, and experts. He then goes on to provide solutions to these problems that slow people from making the progress they desire to run a successful business – ultimately enabling them to live an impactful life. The author's decades of experience are evident in his rich understanding of the topics, along with his insightful delivery. Don't think about it, grab this book now and break down the barriers holding your business back!

Charles Byrd, Evernote Productivity Guru

PUT THIS BOOK INTO PRACTICE, THEN STEP BACK AND WATCH YOUR WHOLE WORLD CHANGE

If you're an advisor, coach, consultant, or trainer, who's tried a lot of techniques and spent a lot of time and money on marketing with mixed-to-awful results, I strongly urge you to open the Kindle version of this book and search for "Here's why the traditional Product Funnel probably won't work for you."

In coaching business owners from start-up through $100M mark, I've seen more service-based companies waste more time, money, and energy on marketing funnels than you would even believe. In SO many cases, it's all been a waste. This is particularly true for business owners who try to mimic info-marketing models.

The author explains not only why this doesn't work, but also how to evaluate your marketing efforts, explains how to properly define your ideal client, step-by-step instructions for crafting an effective message, advises on selecting the effective media, and a number of other critical topics. If you read and implement what the author suggests in this book you'll have done what 95% of marketers have NOT done; you'll have made your marketing as good as your service. And when that happens? Step back and watch your whole world change.

Robert Michon, The Unstoppable CEO

A HIGHLY ACTIONABLE BOOK THAT HELPS YOU CREATE A STRATEGY TO INCREASE LEADS INTO YOUR BUSINESS

I absolutely loved this book. Tom delivers so many practical tips for creating a lead machine. One of my favorites parts of the book is when he goes into the mistakes that we make when we set out to increase our leads. Mistake #12 really hit home, which is lowering prices to increase leads. This was a good reminder that the race to the bottom is not the way to create a lead generating machine and in some cases raising prices actually helps increase lead flow. I highly recommend it to any business owner in need of leads!

Joshua Millage, Entrepreneur and co-founder of Lifter LMS

HELPFUL FOR MY START-UP BUSINESS

I am planning to start my own business and I still have some questions when it comes to finding the right clients for me and how my marketing model should be. Leadsology® has helped me to understand a lot of things, especially in the first chapter about the revenue and the profit and how it should be enough for my chosen lifestyle. This is a really good book to read for people like me who wants to start their own business. It is packed with resources and useful tips that you can actually implement.

Alexandra Karenina Arabelo

AN INSIGHTFUL RESOURCE!

In Leadsology®, Tom Poland offers advisors, coaches, consultants, and trainers a step-by-step Lead Generation Model – one that is beautifully tailored to this audience's specific needs. Grounded in professional experience and observations, Leadsology is written with passion and deep knowledge.
An insightful, elegant, and practical resource – I certainly recommend it.

Dorie Clark, Marketing, Branding and Management Consultant

GREAT MARKETING BOOK FOR SERVICE PROFESSIONALS

This book is a tool chest of easy to use strategies to attract good numbers of high-quality clients. Every chapter has some nuggets of wisdom that are easy to use. Highly recommended.

Graham McGregor, Marketing and sales consultant, trainer, coach

FINALLY!

For anyone who like me is an advisor (or coach or consultant or trainer) and has done the run-around trying to find a genuine specialist in how to message and market our types of service, this is the ultimate answer: Leadsology® is genuinely tailored to us, with tremendous insight that is completely on the mark about us, presented as a simple, proven, step-by-step progressive process you are walked through, hand-in-hand, by a true expert. And it works!

Elizabeth Brown, Branding and Marketing Consultant

SPECIFICALLY FOR COACHES & CONSULTANTS

If you're a coach or consultant who wants more leads, this book is a must read because it's specifically for you.

I've been studying and using direct response marketing since 1997 and this is a great resource to now add to my tool chest!

Kevin Thompson, Marketer, consultant, coach

HOLDS A MIRROR UP TO YOUR MARKETING - AND SHOWS YOU WHERE IT'S UGLY. (THAT'S A GOOD THING)

Tom Poland is clearly gifted at creating a simple-to-understand framework for what it takes to generate leads for your business. I consider myself a marketing professional, and reading through Tom's book gave me good ideas and showed a few places I could improve.

If you're struggling to generate leads in your service business, this book will help you solve that problem.

Frank Bria, Author, Speaker, Strategist

PRACTICAL AND EFFECTIVE LEAD GENERATION SYSTEM

Leadsology® is a practical, effective and implementable system that helps you create a predictable flow of high quality inbound new client inquiries into your business. Tom's book and system will show you how to stop random acts of marketing and get you back in the driver's seat running your business. You can easily swipe and deploy his 10-step lead generation model so that you can work smart not harder.

This is a great book for advisors and consultants to learn how to create a system that brings in a predictable flow of clients and shows you how best to invest your marketing time. I have had the privilege of working with the author and have been so pleased with the results and the practical, effective and easy to implement nature of this model which is all laid out in the book. I definitely recommend this book.

Susan Kleinschmidt, Consultant, Trainer Coach

COOL NEW LEAD GENERATION ROADMAP FOR SERVICE AND ADVISORY PROFESSIONALS

Not to toot my own horn, but I've been an internationally recognized expert on Sales, Lead Generation and Positioning for many years now, so I know a thing or two about great lead-generation systems.

There are tons of books out there about lead gen, but what's different with this book is that it's especially written for folks who specialize in service and/or advisory businesses, and NOT for those who sell physical products.

They say that specificity is power and I believe that the advisor-specific strategies in this book are what makes it so powerful. Tom's book truly "disrupts" the status quo, and offers a road map that will lead you to generate a consistent flow of high quality, inbound leads.

Buy this book. Implement every suggestion. Then sit back and watch the new clients flow into your business.

Erik Luhrs, GURU Selling System

PAVING THE ROAD TO SUCCESS

For coaches, trainers and consultants like me, it is often challenging to balance delivery and marketing, to find new clients while servicing established ones, to have such a finely tuned business model in place that it creates ongoing high quality inquiries.

The comprehensive ten-step Leadsology® model outlined in this book helped me to get clear about the what, the where, the when and the how. The structure, the suggestions and guidelines, they all make sense.

With over 35 years of experience, Tom knows what he is talking about. His clarity and wisdom shine through every story, every comprehensive model and concept that are clearly only so simple because Tom has done all the work.

I also really appreciate the honesty and candor with which he points out likely pitfalls, especially poignant when they are the ones I already fell into. If you want to grow your business and have a good life to boost, read this book - and then work with Tom.

Angela Heise, Trainer, consultant, coach

A TREASURE TROVE OF INFORMATION

Leadsology® is a treasure trove of information not only about lead generation, but also about how to wire our whole business for success. Tom Poland's 10-part model for being in demand is a comprehensive summary of all the elements we need to have optimized for our business to be coasting along like a well-oiled wheel.

There are so many gems of information in this book, that if we even take one, and implement it, it makes a difference. I know that I've already changed my marketing message because of this, and people are much more interested in what I do now. There is also a surprising departure from the normal way of structuring online marketing – specifically for what Tom calls "advisors." This is vital information that could be the one thing that brings advisors the revenues and number of clients we are really looking for.

Glenda Nicholls, Founder, Money Success System

LEAD GENERATION: NOW A SIMPLE AND ELEGANT SCIENCE

Many of us employ a very hit-and-miss approach to marketing and lead generation – with very hit-and-miss results. With "Leadsology®" however, Tom Poland has turned lead generation into a science that is both simple and elegant.

In a market where we've all got used to the same old marketing formula, Tom brings a fresh approach that provides cut through in a noisy world. You'll enjoy the easy-to-implement, step-by-step approach outlined in this book.

And, I have no doubt, you'll enjoy the results this unique system can generate.

Dawn Russell, Founder of Heartwired, trainer and coach

ABOUT THE AUTHOR

Tom Poland is the creator of the proprietary Leadsology® Model and works with professionals to embed lead-generation systems into their businesses so they enjoy a weekly flow of new client inquiries.

Tom started his first advisory business at age 24 and has gone on to start and sell four others, taking two of them international. In that time, he's managed teams of over 100 people and annual revenue of more than $20 million.

He has published four books and also shared international speaking platforms with the likes of Michael Gerber of *E-Myth* fame, Richard Koch from *The 80–20 Principle*, Marshall Goldsmith and many others.

Tom is voluntarily married and lives on the sand at Castaways Beach on the fabulous Sunshine Coast of Queensland, Australia.

Contents

INTRODUCTION

I**T'S SAID THAT** nothing happens in a business until something is sold.

And while that's true, nothing is sold until a lead is generated.

Effective marketing generates a flow of high quality, inbound (very important word), new client inquiries, predictably and systematically, like turning on a tap and enjoying the benefits of flowing water.

And in much the same way that life would cease to exist without water, without new client inquiries, professional services businesses also would die.

And that's why this book is so important: to help professionals sustain and thrive in their businesses.

Further, this book needed to be written and it needed to be written specifically for professionals offering services, advice, or software, for five reasons.

FIRST: Effective marketing is very different for professionals Marketing The Invisible than it is for those marketing the physical.

Professionals trying to transfer effective marketing strategies deployed in the world of physical products to the world of the intangible are doomed to failure, because the former is a relationship decision and the latter is a transaction decision. It's the difference between proposing marriage and buying a washing machine.

Because of that fact, this book shows you how to take a potentially ideal client from a state of being unaware of you, to one where they quite literally regard you as their highest-quality option for overcoming their challenge, and fervently hope they might be able to work with you.

SECOND: Professionals looking for marketing help are subject to an avalanche of offers from either well-meaning-but-ineffective advisors, or from the charlatans who are far better at the razzle-dazzle of selling than they are at delivering real value.

This book subjects the recommended methods of both categories of advisors to the harsh and bright lights of reality, exposing the mistruths and misinformation that are unfortunately almost universally preached, then flogged off as an effective solution.

THIRD: Almost everyone you turn to for marketing advice will have one method they offer you.

It might be SEO or AdWords; it might be Facebook advertising; it might be online funnels; it might be LinkedIn; it might be running events; it might be webinars or Facebook groups or writing a book or creating landing pages or producing videos and so on.

But when all you have is a hammer, suddenly, everything looks like a nail.

For example, if you find yourself in a conversation with someone who offers a course on how to use webinars to generate clients, then not surprisingly they'll tell you, almost every single time, that webinars are the very best thing you can do to generate new clients.

And if you find yourself talking to a SEO and landing pages expert, then likewise, they'll tell you that it would be an excellent idea for you to invest with them so they can start generating clients for you using SEO and landing pages.

And the same would apply if you are speaking to someone who sells Facebook advertising services, or who was marketing a program on how to generate clients through physical events, and so on.

To paraphrase the aforementioned truism: when all you have is a webinar, suddenly everyone looks like a registrant.

So who's right? Where do you begin? Which is the best strategy for generating new clients?

The answer is that it depends on your specific type of service/advice/software, and it also depends on the market that you want to generate leads from.

You must match the medium to the market, otherwise it doesn't work. Offering webinars to CEOs is like me putting a bunch of flowers in my dog's dinner bowl. At best, you'll get ignored and at worst you're in danger of being sprayed on by your intended Audience.

In summary, it's very rare that you can trust someone who has only one method for generating new clients, because it's very likely that their advice will be skewed in favor of you buying whatever it is they are selling, because that's all they have to offer.

And that brings me very nicely to the **fourth reason** that this book had to be written.

Setting up a system to generate a stream of new leads might sound like a worthy goal, but it's not; it has a fundamental flaw at its core.

That's because, if you are your household's main financial rainmaker, then the financial security and prosperity of your family depends on your ability to generate new clients.

And if you only have one method of generating new client inquiries, then your family is in a position of great financial insecurity and vulnerability.

Someone once said that the number one is the scariest number in business.

One main client, one main supplier, one key staff member — it all adds up to the same thing, which is that your financial future is vulnerable to one thing changing.

And it's the same thing with lead generation: you don't need a stream of new leads, you need multiple streams of new leads because the diversity of flow gives you both security and prosperity.

And finally, the **fifth** reason this book had to be written is that you are not Hugh Jackman (or the female equivalent).

The other morning over coffee I asked my wife who she thought was the sexiest, more irresistible man alive.

(And yes, I knew this could be entering unnecessarily dangerous territory.)

"Why of course, you are sweetie," Petal said, grinning in a way that you just know it ain't true.

(Petal is my cutie-pie name for her. You have to call her Ute – pronounced "oo-ta")

"Yes, I know I am, I mean who could resist my bald head, pot belly and wrinkled skin? But apart from me?"

She came up with a few names like Roger Federer (Petal is a tennis fan) and George Clooney, but I didn't see any spark in her eyes, so I kept pressing her.

"There must be someone else," I persisted, "someone that's so irresistible that he's as close as anyone is going to get to be the proverbial God's Gift to Women."

"Ah!" she cried, "I've got it! Hugh Jackman!"

"Of course!" I agreed. "He can sing, he can dance, he can act, he's a devoted husband and family man, apparently deeply caring about all sorts of social and environmental issues. He's incredibly good-looking and he's got a body that would make Adonis jealous. Plus, he's got enough money for the next 100 lifetimes."

Petal's face suddenly looked flushed and she started waving both hands frantically at her cheeks in a futile attempt to make them a lighter shade of crimson and to cool the small beads of sweat spontaneously breaking out on her forehead.

That's when I knew that we had a winner. Congrats to Mr. Jackman.

"OK," I said. "I've got another question for you.

Imagine that there's a knock at the front door right now. You put down your coffee, go to the door, and you open it. And it's Hugh Jackman. He sees you, drops to one knee, and holds up a small box and opens it to reveal a million -diamond ring and the first words out of his mouth are 'Hi Ute, I'm Hugh Jackman. I know we've never met before, but would you make me the happiest man on earth by marrying me, and come and live with me for the rest of your life?'

What would you say to him?" I asked.

"Well firstly'" she said, "you know that I love you, right?"

"Sure" I said, "I know that you love me."

"And second, and I'm sorry to tell you this, but you also know that you'd never see me again, right?"

"Petal, there is absolutely no need to apologize," I said. "Frankly, if I'd answered the door, and Hugh was on bended knee proposing to me, I'd have probably said yes too."

Anyhoo, back to you, my valued reader.

So, what's Hugh Jackman proposing to my beautiful wife (whom after much counseling, I have forgiven), got to do with you and your marketing?

Plenty.

Most people practice what I call Hugh Jackman Marketing.

They conduct their marketing as if what they have is so irresistible, so incredible, so genius-filled, that everyone they meet should instantly want to do business with them.

For example: they go to a business networking meeting with the intent of "picking up" a new client. They thrust their business cards into the hands of people they've never met before, hoping that one of them will want to work with them.

For example: they put an advertisement in a paper or magazine or online, promoting their services and hoping someone will read it and immediately make contact and inquire about becoming a client.

For example: they hope that they sit next to a high-quality prospect at their next dinner party so they'll be able to woo that person into becoming a client.

I call this Hugh Jackman Marketing because they think that they can get to an "engagement" on their first meeting. Or second or third.

Either way it comes down to the same approach: a failure to allow a prospect to get to know your work and to progressively discover how awesome you are "on the inside" because, let's face it, most of us do not possess the business equivalent of Hugh Jackman's irresistibility and our potential Ideal Clients may just need a few "dates" first to see that true beauty is more than just skin deep.

Enter Jack Hughman. (Please read that twice: it's not Hugh Jackman).

Yes, Jack Hughman really exists and in fact, as of 37 minutes ago, he's became a first level connection with me on LinkedIn.

Whereas Hugh Jackman flies around the world in his private jet, singing, dancing, and acting on some of the world's biggest stages, Jack Hughman is the manager of Nando's chicken restaurant in Doncaster, South Yorkshire, postcode 7NW, in the UK.

And if you check out his LinkedIn profile, you'll see that Jack Hughman is just a wee little bit short of looking quite as handsome as his malapropistic counterpart, Hugh Jackman.

Just a bit.

Actually, sorry Jack, but quite a lot.

Anyhoo, back to the reason why I want to tell you about Jack Hughman.

(And please refrain from connecting with him on LinkedIn and telling him about this book and commenting on the twist of fate that had him born Jack Hughman and not Hugh Jackman, because I don't want to worry about a knock at the front door from a rather large and very angry South Yorkshireman).

But despite looking like he may have sampled one too many Nando banquets, Jack Hughman appears to be a lovely bloke.

And while I don't really know him personally, let's assume that he's the sort of guy that any woman would be lucky to have.

Loyal, kind, caring, and most certainly a very good provider, in the form of a seemingly endless supplier of legendary flame-grilled PERi-PERi chicken burgers and lukewarm French fries.

But despite those many admirable attributes, if it was Jack Hughman, and not Hugh Jackman, on one knee when my wife opened the door, I'm pretty sure he'd have the door slammed in his face (probably immediately after she snatched the diamond ring out of his hand) and he'd be on his bike, so to speak.

At the very least, to wrest my wife away from me, Jack Hughman would have to take her on a few dates first... but let's not go there, in the unlikely event that my wife ever reads this book.

(Quick tip for Jack: it's probably best not to take Petal to Nando's on the first date).

But back to you.

I want to encourage you to do your marketing as if, metaphorically speaking, your service is less like Hugh Jackman and more like Jack Hughman.

In other words, be patient. Let your prospects get to know you and don't make the mistake of premature proposition.

According to my website stats, the average new client has experienced my brand five times before they buy.

And we (the client and me) may have had a webinar "date" together, dated during my **www.FiveHourChallenge.com** together, dated over a book of mine (me writing, them reading) together... and so on.

And that's the big difference between Marketing The Invisible and marketing a physical product: you need to allow people to get to know you and trust you before you pop the question.

Patience my friend.

All good things come to him and her who sit... and market their butt off.

More to be revealed soon....

So, there you have it: the five reasons why this book was written:

1. Because Marketing The Invisible requires a different approach to marketing the physical.

2. Because the marketplace abounds with misinformation about how to generate new clients.

3. Because almost everyone you turn to for marketing help will offer their solution as the best solution, if not the only solution, to meet your lead-generation needs.

4. And because a stream of leads is not enough; for the sake of your future security and prosperity, you need multiple streams of leads.

5. You and I are not quite the marketing equivalent of my wife being proposed to by Hugh Jackman (I'm sure she would have said no. Probably.)

THIS BOOK'S CORE MESSAGE AND IMPORTANT FOUNDATION KNOWLEDGE FOR EFFECTIVE LEAD GENERATION

Why I Wrote This Book and Who It's for

G<small>REETINGS.</small>

It's probably clear from the cover of this book that I wrote it for professionals who offer either a service, advice, or software and who want to enjoy a predictable flow of high-quality, inbound, new client inquiries.

THE CORE MESSAGE OF THIS BOOK

Continuing that theme, the core message of this book is that, if you are a professional and the main money-winner in your household, then you can and must embed multiple streams of leads into your business so that your financial future and that of your family is not only secure, but prosperous.

However, what may not be quite so clear from the cover is *why* I wrote the book. It's actually very important that you understand my motivations because it provides you with the potential to make a lot more money if you ever write your own book, or indeed if you ever present to an Audience full of your ideal clients.

And if it were possible, I'd to be willing to bet that you've never read another author give the same reason for writing a book as I'm about to give you.

First though, a little backgrounder…

One of the clarion calls you'll hear throughout this book is the need for marketers (and very soon I hope that you realize this includes you) to stop being sneaky and to start putting some integrity and authenticity back into how we go about convincing people that they should work with us, rather than someone else.

I'm making that call because there is a ubiquitous, pervasive, and prevalent notion that's resident in the thinking of professional and amateur marketers alike, that we need to be tricky, manipulative, and devious to convince people that they should do business with us.

That manipulative style of marketing attempts to bend our Audience's mind to our point of view with less than honest methodology and has its origins in the idea that the more effective marketers must bend their ethics out of shape.

It's like people who have something to sell are thinking: *"tell me the formula for getting new clients and, if need be, I'll twist my personality to be whoever I have to be, and I'll bend my values and ethics out of whack too, so long as I get the new clients flowing in."*

When in fact, there could be no approach that's further from what we need to do in order to market the invisible effectively.

The only difference between obtaining money by deceitful marketing and achieving the same objective through honest marketing is the lack of a truthful, creative idea.

I am therefore compelled, by my own declaration of honest intent, to let you know right up front that the primary reason I wrote this book is to convince you that transferring money from your bank account to my bank account is a really good idea...

(...for both of us.)

Now before you drop this book and run away screaming, please understand that you will receive more than full value from your wise investment in my little manuscript, whether we work together or not.

In fact, I'm going to show you, with a level of detail never-before disclosed other than to high fee-paying private clients, how to generate a weekly flow of inbound calendar bookings from highly qualified prospects who want to talk with you about working with you.

And these wise people will make their bookings even though they know how (reassuringly) expensive your fees are.

And the bookings will come in even while you're asleep or on holiday.

Does that sound like a good plan?

I'm betting dollars to donuts that you think it is.

So now that I've reassured you, let's return to my potentially harmful declaration that my primary motivation for writing this book is to convince you that handing your hard-earned cash over to me would be one of the best business decisions that you've ever made.

Frankly, getting new clients on board is THE reason why virtually everyone in a professional services business writes a book.

It's about self-promotion, but few authors seem prepared to come out and say that right up front.

And self-promotion is not such a bad idea. It's not like anyone else is going to do it for us, right?

But let's not kid ourselves, all the other reasons that people give for writing a book like this one... reasons such as *"I'm passionate about [insert name of service here,]*, or *"I just want to give back,"* or *"I want to leave a legacy"* et cetera ... are at worst disingenuous, or at best secondary motivations.

Of course, there are other reasons that I wrote this book.

For example: yes, I like that royalty check each month.

And yes, my heart momentarily skips a happy beat when I'm flying to speak at a conference and, after a bit of pre-flight banter, the guy or gal sitting next to me finds out I'm a writer and turns to me with their face lit up and says "Oh, so you're THAT Tom Poland!"

(Unfortunately, they are normally thinking of my namesake from Augusta, Georgia, who writes most elegantly about the Southern USA).

And yes, there's a part of me that, in the quite moments when I'm not checking my bank balance, really likes the idea of making my little corner of the world a better place.

But most of all, I want you to (quite wisely) give me your money so that I can return the favor multitudinously by spending time with you embedding lead generation systems into your business and training you on how to sustain a flow of new clients in perpetuity.

I mentioned that the revelation of my true motivation is potentially damaging for me, but I should also point out that, as damaging as it could be for me, it has equal potential to be beneficial for you.

That's because by setting an opening tone that is genuine, transparent, honest, and authentic, you're more likely to rightly believe that what follows is a continuation of the same theme and, thereby, pay close attention to my recommendations.

And when you pay close attention to my recommendations, you're far more likely to take the next step of implementing them and thereby gaining a benefit that is exponentially greater than the relatively minor investment of buying this book and/or working with me.

Thus, both my primary mission of legally siphoning money from your bank account and my secondary mission of making your part of the world a slightly better place through better marketing, will both be realized.

And because of my disclosure, you'll receive even more benefit from this book than normal, because now that you know why I wrote it, you'll be able to understand the purpose behind the careful sequencing in the book which follows the Leadsology© Persuasion Sequence I lay out for you in Part Four.

And with those insights you'll more easily be able to "swipe and deploy" the structure I'm using for your own publications and presentations.

So, let me just pause for a moment to thank you for that opportunity.

THANK YOU!

WHAT'S DIFFERENT ABOUT THIS BOOK

There are literally thousands of books about marketing that you could have chosen to read.

And indeed, you may be aware of my previous best-seller "Leadsology®: The Science of Being In Demand," and you may have even read it.

So, the question of what is different about this book is relevant for other books on marketing and for weighing it against my previous book on the same subject.

So, first I'll address what's different in this book versus most other books, and then I'll address the issue of what's different about this book against my previous one.

WHY THIS BOOK IS DIFFERENT FROM OTHER BOOKS ON THE SAME SUBJECT

The biggest difference is that this book offers no Simple, Easy, Fast and Effective solutions.

And before you throw this book away, I want to assure you that it is chock full of the Effective, but it is unashamedly bereft of any promise to combine the idea of Effectiveness with the concepts of Simple, Easy and Fast.

But let's imagine for a moment that you have a magic wand and that you could wave it and make your lead generation wish list come true.

If that were the case, then you'd probably want the following characteristics to be inherent in your marketing methods:

1. Effective

2. Easy

3. Fast

4. Simple

5. Scalable (less dependent on your personal time, with exponentially greater results)

Item #1 probably goes without saying, although judging by the number of people who pay good money to learn *ineffective* lead-generation methods, it's probably worth mentioning.

Item #2 on our list above is possible, although not in the short term.

That's because lead generation is like any other skill. When you start trying to develop a new skill such as tennis or playing the piano or learning a foreign language, it's not easy.

And an underlying theme in this book, and indeed the way that I work with clients, is that I want to not only give you the lead generation systems, but also train you in their principles and operation, so that you are equipped to generate leads even in the inevitable changing times to come.

It's an old cliché (tired but true), that I want to not simply give you a fish, but teach you how to catch them.

But back to item #2 above. You can take comfort in the fact that everything is hard until it's Easy.

The trick is to start. The journey of 1,000 miles and so on. Another cliché, but again very true.

So yes, if you are prepared to make the commitment to implement the strategies contained in this book, then what you may find is that what was difficult to start with will become Easy with practice.

As for item #3 on our wish list, you can generate leads Fast, but only after you've done the "slow" work of building lead generation *systems*.

For example, one of the lead-generation systems that I'll reveal In Part Three took me nine months of testing, measuring, and failing before I perfected it.

Having now documented and systematized the process, a new client will typically take less than 30 days to customize and embed the system into their business, and then they will be able to generate leads week after week, ad infinitum.

So "Fast" is a bit like "Easy" in that it's possible, but only after you've done the work of developing the system. Once you got that, then you've got lead generation leverage.

In summary so far, everyone wants "Effective."

And "Easy", together with "Fast", *are* possible, but only after you've invested time in developing the skills and systems.

This book will help with both of those.

That brings us to item # 4: Simple.

Simple marketing that generates leads is either extraordinarily inefficient from a time point of view (e.g. business networking meetings) or is incredibly inefficient financially (e.g. sending out 10,000 direct mail pieces) or is both inefficient and ineffective (e.g. cold-calling or paid media advertising).

But is it possible for your marketing to be Simple?

The answer is yes, but it can't be Simple as well as Efficient and Effective.

The concept of Simple and Effective/Efficient are mutually exclusive when it comes to marketing.

There is an exception, however.

And that exception is where you follow a proven, step-by-step system, one that's been developed by someone else and where that someone else trains you in that system.

And yes, that observation may appear to be self-serving, given that I market such systems. But it also happens to be the truth.

That's why franchise businesses comprise the largest business category by number, globally.

Because someone has taken the time and trouble to make running a complex business a simpler process, by creating proven step-by-step systems that they then train the franchisee to run.

Finally, we have item #5 on your wish list, Scalable.

I use the term Scalable to refer to your ability to generate an increasing number of leads without a commensurate increase in the expenditure of your time.

I'll discuss this in more detail In Part Six, but for now let me just say that Scalability is at the heart of Leadsology® and that it's 100 percent _incompatible_ with a desire for anything that is Simple, Fast and Easy all at the same time.

At this point, I need to sincerely invite anyone who still believes that lead generation should be simultaneously effective, fast, easy, simple and scalable to go back to **www.Amazon.com** and search for a different book.

The book _How To Pray For Miracles_ might be a good place to start!

My methods are initially not Easy, Fast and Simple.

BUT I WILL PROMISE YOU THIS...

Implement my methods, be observant and patient, and fine-tune them when necessary.

Then you will be waking up most mornings delighted to see fresh bookings in your calendar made by people who would be ideal clients and who want to talk about working with you.

HOW THIS BOOK IS DIFFERENT FROM MY PREVIOUS BOOK

Writing a second book on the same subject presents something of a dilemma.

On the one hand I want to make certain that anyone who has not read my last book is able to gain an understanding of the key foundation concepts presented in the previous book so that they can receive full value from this one, without having to read the previous one.

On the other hand, I want to make sure that all the readers who helped to make my last book a best-seller don't find a lot of repetition in this new book.

Therefore, to make sure that both the new and repeat readers are all deliriously happy with their investment in this book, I'm going to borrow from the previous book quite scantily and only when necessary.

To paraphrase Einstein: "repeat enough, but not enougher" ☺

Naturally, if you have not read my previous book "Leadsology®: The Science of Being In Demand" then I'd be delighted if you pop onto **www.Amazon.com** and check it out. But you really should only read it after this one for the purpose of understanding key concepts such as The Value Slider (how to make a service significantly more attractive to your ideal client), The Poland Calendar (how to easily and simply get all the time you need to do your marketing) and to gain an introduction to the other six parts of the Leadsology® Model not covered in this book.

It's worth mentioning, however, that my previous book laid out a 10-part model that professionals can use to gain an overview of how to generate a weekly flow of high-quality, inbound, new client inquiries.

You can download a free copy of that model at: **www.leadsology.guru/the-model/**

As mentioned, this book is a continuation of the same theme of showing professionals how to generate inbound leads. However, it focuses almost exclusively on the first four parts of the previously mentioned 10-part model by diving deeper into each of those specialist areas.

To achieve that "deep dive," this book introduces a considerable number of new concepts, methods, and principles including:

THE TITANIUM TRIANGLE which shows you how to create an indestructible flow of new clients.

THE LEADSOLOGY® PERSUASION SEQUENCE, which lays out a cunningly effective 10-step model for convincing your ideal clients to work with you. You can adopt this for use in your presentations, productions, and pitches.

THE FOUR STAGES OF PSYCHOLOGICAL ALLURE which demonstrates exactly how to have your Ideal Clients not just wanting to work with you but determined to do so.

THE S.E.W. SEGMENTATION FORMULA that lays out for you a simple but proven effective method for multiplying the number of new client inquiries five-fold.

Note: I am aware that some of the claims I make above may seem extravagant and therefore at odds with my previously stated intention of keeping things real. So please rest assured that I have chosen every word very carefully and that I sincerely mean each and every one of those words. That said, it would be worth reading the above four paragraphs once again because the promises inherent within them are truly some of the most remarkably powerful marketing methodologies that you are likely to encounter.

WHAT THIS BOOK IS AND WHAT IT IS NOT

Sadly, this book cannot be all things to all people.

But it can be a lot of things to a lot of people.

To help explain what you can and cannot expect from this book, I'll use an analogy drawn from my passion for the game of tennis.

Imagine for a moment that you have never played tennis, but that you watch a match between two champions and are suddenly inspired to learn the game.

So off you go to a bookstore and you buy the very best book you can on the game of tennis.

You learn the language of forehand topspin, backhand slice, Continental versus Western grips and so on.

A great book is a terrific way to start learning how to play a great game of tennis.

But it's not a training manual and the words on the pages of even a great book cannot take the place of a human being who can coach you on how to take the words that you read and embed them in your mind in such a way that you are able to play a great game of tennis.

There is absolutely no doubt that you are better off in buying and reading that great book.

And there is also absolutely no doubt that it's not enough on its own.

Hopefully, you'll agree this book is like that great book on how to play tennis. Having read it, you'll have significantly advanced your potential to play the game of lead generation.

You'll have been introduced to new and proven-effective methods and techniques, just like a great book on tennis will do.

Your mind will have been opened to new possibilities and potential and, indeed, your thinking will have been positively advanced and broadened.

But what this book cannot do is to take the place of an in-depth training course, complete with step-by-step systems, and, unfortunately, it also cannot take the place of you wisely investing in a human being who can coach you how to take the words on the pages of this book, and embed them into your business in such a way that you're playing a great game of lead generation.

And again, in line with my intention to be transparent, genuine and honest with you, that is simply the reality of books.

It's like that old saying: "the map is not the territory."

That being the case, you can bet your bottom dollar that if I were to attempt a death-defying climb of one of the world's deadliest mountains, I'll sure as heck be taking a map and studying it very carefully. I'll also find a guide to climb with me.

Which is exactly what I recommend that you do with this book: find a course and a guide to help you reach your lead generation goal as swiftly and certainly as possible.

Part One:

PREPARING YOUR MIND FOR LEAD GENERATION MAGIC (CRITICAL!)

The Core Message of this Book

IN **THE INTRODUCTION** to this book I mentioned the old saying *"nothing happens in a business until something is sold."*

What is meant by that is that, until a sale is made, there is no money to deliver services, no employee can be paid, suppliers can't be satisfied, lease obligations cannot be fulfilled, no advertising can be booked, and so on.

But as also mentioned earlier, while it may be true that nothing happens in a business until something is sold, nothing is sold until a lead is generated.

Think of that lead as the first in a series of dominoes.

Doubtless you've seen some sort of record attempt whereby a person sets up many thousands of dominoes, one in front of another, and then simply tips over the first domino and you watch in awe as the others fall over one by one.

Think of those many dominoes as being important, financially influenced aspects of your life.

Once you generate a new client inquiry, that's like the first domino tipping over.

The next domino that tips over is you bringing a new client on board.

That tips over the cash-flow domino.

That tips over the domino that allows you to pay all your suppliers on time.

That tips over the domino that allows you to take cash out of your business and improve the quality of the home you have made, and it allows you greater choice in where you live, in the mountains or next to the beach or on a quiet ranch in the desert.

There are other dominoes for your sports, hobbies, and philanthropic pursuits.

And there are dominoes that support your children's education and that allow your husband/wife/partner the time and freedom to pursue their passion.

And as a professional provider of a service or advice or software, every single one of those dominoes is dependent on your ability to knock over that very first domino of generating a new client inquiry.

Most professionals rely on word of mouth marketing to knock over that first domino.

That's scary for two closely related reasons.

First, to think that so many of the quality choices in your life have been left to random chance is not something that would comfort any right-thinking or completely sane person.

Second, as you'll discover in part three of this book, having only one source of new clients is like regularly betting your house on a pair of twos in poker.

You might win that bet once or even twice, but it is absolutely and inarguably inevitable that you will eventually lose that bet.

In writing about the core message of this book, I need to also add that far too many professionals are like the world's proverbial "best kept secret," in that they are brilliant at what they do, but they suck at marketing what they do so their full potential to make their part of the world a better place is sadly never realized.

So, the core message of this book can be summed up as follows:

To be able to relax and fulfill your professional potential, as well as enjoy the peace of mind and security that comes from an abundance of cash, you must embed multiple streams for leads within your business.

AN INTRODUCTION TO LEADSOLOGY®

I'll give you a deeper insight into the nature of Leadsology® with an analogy.

Imagine a forest that's full of Grizzly Bears and those bears all happen to be asleep.

And imagine that you have a pot of honey and you really want the bears to eat your honey.

In this analogy, the bears are a metaphor for your potential clients, and the honey is a metaphor for your service, advice, or software.

You want the bears to eat your honey, just as you want clients to consume your service.

You have a couple of options to achieve your objective.

The first option is to find a very large stick with a sharp point and then go running through the forest finding sleeping bears and jabbing it in their backside so they wake up.

Having poked a bear, you then wave your pot of honey under the nose of the very aggravated animal and hope like hell their hunger level exceeds their anger level.

If you're lucky, the bear decides to consume the honey, and not you.

But if you're unlucky... well, let's not go there.

This first part of my metaphor is analogous to what people do when they send out 10,000 direct mail pieces, or cold-call 100 people, or trot down to business networking meetings and thrust their business card into the hands of all and sundry.

In every one of those examples, the perpetrator has absolutely no idea which of the people they are inflicting themselves upon, if any, have an interest in their service.

Even worse, that same perpetrator is hoping against hope that the one in 1,000 people who may be interested in what they're spruiking will perceive them to be the supplier of first choice, even though they've interrupted their day with an uninvited "prodding."

Frankly, it's far more likely that they'll be perceived as one of many other suppliers, all involved in a "Dance of the Desperate," and will be far more turned off by the idea of working with that person than they are turned on by the same thought.

And in addition to the one in 1,000 who may be a prospect but who was turned off to the idea of working with that stick-wielding person, there are the additional 999 who, like the bears who preferred to continue sleeping, are simply annoyed by having been disturbed.

The second option is much more effective: you simply take your honey pot and place it outside of the forest.

The sleeping bears will catch whiff of the honey and the hungry ones will probably start dreaming that they are swimming in honey, then wake up feeling a little disappointed until they realize that there is in fact a real honey pot to be found.

Those bears will have qualified themselves as being high-quality prospects for your honey and they will walk, if not run, out of the forest, and eagerly consume your honey.

And that's what Leadsology® does: it has highly qualified prospects seeking you out in the form of using your online scheduling link to book a time to talk with you about becoming a client.

And just like putting a honey pot outside a forest, and then walking away, all of this will happen regardless of whether you are at work, on holiday, awake, or sleeping.

And those highly qualified prospects will be making that booking already aware of what your fees are and how you work with clients.

In summary, Leadsology® is all about generating inbound (keyword), qualified, new client inquiries in a manner that is predictable because of its systematic nature.

WHAT LEADSOLOGY® IS NOT

Now you have a clear understanding of what Leadsology® is, but I want to add to that clarity by briefly describing what it is not.

Here's a list of things that are excluded in every Leadsology® lead generation system:

- Manipulative sales techniques
- Cold-calling
- Mass direct mail letter drops
- Hype and BS copywriting
- Complicated online funnel advertising
- Paid media advertising
- Stalking people on LinkedIn
- Expecting to generate new client inquiries from Social Media
- Attending business networking meetings
- Submitting tenders
- Crazy stacked bonus offers (Ginsu Steak Knives anyone?)
- Discounting of services
- Hiring "appointment setters"
- Affiliate marketing
- Online advertising

At the risk of stating the obvious, the above list excludes almost all the traditional marketing methods taught by many publicly recognized sales and marketing experts.

Which begs the question: "if Leadsology® doesn't engage in any of those things, how the heck am I to go about generating any leads?"

That's a great question, but for now I'm going to have to beg your patience and ask you to sit on that question until we get to Part Three, where I will be much more specific about the exact lead generation methods that *will* work well for you as a professional provider of a service, advice, or software.

The reason I'm asking you to bide your time before you get to that answer is that the information I'm laying out for you in this book throughout the Preface and Parts One and Two are sequenced very carefully so that you'll gain maximum advantage from my more specific recommendations in Part Three.

In other words, if you skip straight to Part Three, you'll be doing yourself a grave disservice in terms of your ability to maximize the value of my specific lead generation recommendations contained that section of the book.

So hang in there!

YOUR NUMBER ONE PROBLEM AND YOUR NUMBER ONE NUMBER

You have a problem.

And aside from this problem, you really don't have any other problems.

What I mean by that is that, once you crack this problem, almost all your other problems will either disappear or become better-quality problems.

The problems that will disappear are related to funding your ideal home in your ideal location, funding other lifestyle choices such as holidays and the pursuit of passion pastimes including hobbies sports and philanthropic causes and so on.

And one of the problems will transform from a poor-quality problem into a high-quality problem.

More specifically, the poor-quality problem of not having a systematized and therefore predictable flow of high-quality new client inquiries will transform into the high-quality problem of having too many clients to service.

That's what effective lead generation does: it ramps up demand for your services and in doing so dramatically improves your revenue as well as lifestyle choices.

Too much demand is a quality problem. And that's a problem which I'm delighted to be able to show you how to create.

But let's get back to looking at your current problem.

The classic way of defining a problem is to figure out the difference between what you've got and what you want.

For example, if on average you're currently bringing two new clients on board each month and you really want five new clients each month, then your problem can be defined as three new clients a month.

And let's say that you convert a very modest 50 percent of qualified new client inquiries into new clients.

If that's the case, then we can get even more specific about what your problem looks like by working backwards from your goal of three new clients a month and saying that, in fact, your problem is six new qualified leads per month.

That number of six new qualified leads per month becomes what I call your Number One Number.

In this example, six new leads become the pre-eminent objective and the dominating thought in your business life, because once you defeat that problem and you're regularly generating those six new leads, all your other problems either disappear or transform from low-quality problems into high-quality problems, as outlined above.

THE SYMPTOMS OF YOUR PROBLEM, THE CAUSE AND THE SOLUTION

In the example above, we defined your problem as being six new leads per month.

Anyone who has a lead generation problem will be experiencing at least three symptoms.

See if you can relate to one or more of these symptoms.

SYMPTOM NUMBER ONE IS ANXIETY

If you don't have the security of a regular flow of high-quality new client inquiries, then the chances are you'll feel stressed about how to pay the bills, where your next client is coming from, how you can fund the next vacation, where the money is going to come from for your children's education and so on.

You might feel Anxiety in the form of frustration. People sometimes feel frustrated when they see competitors who offer an inferior service doing better than they are, often simply because they are doing better marketing.

Anxiety can also come in the form of disappointment. This is quite common if you know that you have something that can transform businesses/lives, yet you remain a "best-kept secret."

SYMPTOM NUMBER TWO IS RANDOM ACTS OF MARKETING

Random Acts of Marketing is sponsored by the Anxiety mentioned above.

You wake up one morning, having tossed and turned half the night worried about where your next client is going to come from, and you resolve to take action.

You search for local business networking meetings, or you call ex-clients saying you want to catch up for a coffee (and you know that they know it's a pretense, and that what you're really doing is flagging that you're short of work), or you decide to venture into the world of Facebook advertising (which you figure you can do for around $20 a day so, hey, why not give it a whirl?), or you put your head down and bum up and write an article that you think is pure genius and post it on LinkedIn.

My American friends have a saying that goes something like this "even a blind squirrel will find an acorn in a forest once in a while."

And yes, your Random Acts of Marketing may occasionally produce a new client.

But I want to ask you the same question that Clint Eastwood's Dirty Harry asked the thug robbing the convenience store, with eyes squinting down the barrel of a Magnum 44 in the direction of said thug: *"I only have one question for you: do ya feel lucky today? Well, do ya — punk?"*

So, do you feel lucky?

Or would you prefer to rely on a systematic approach that produces a predictable flow of high-quality, inbound, new client inquiries?

Of course, that's a rhetorical question because I know the answer because you've invested in this book.

Good for you, because you picked the right answer, which is to embed proven lead generation systems into your business so that you can be financially secure and professionally fulfilled because the acorns come looking for you.

SYMPTOM NUMBER THREE IS ROLLERCOASTER REVENUE

Just as Random Acts of Marketing was triggered by Anxiety, Rollercoaster Revenue is triggered by Random Acts of Marketing.

By necessity, rollercoasters take you on a journey that goes up and down. That's why people ride them, for the thrill of hurtling downward at high speeds.

I'm pretty sure though that, when it comes to your cash flow, you'd prefer not to find yourself screaming as you plunge at high speed toward a bank balance that reads zero.

But that's exactly what happens when Anxiety sponsors Random Acts of Marketing: one month you have plenty of work and strong cash flow, but the next, both of those commodities have disappeared.

WHY MARKETING THE INVISIBLE REQUIRES A DIFFERENT APPROACH TO MARKETING THE PHYSICAL

I find a lot of confusion among people when it comes to marketing their services. The confusion is caused by over-information and miss-information.

We're subjected to a bombardment of paid advertising and, because of the programming effect that experience has on our mind, it's easy to begin thinking that the way to generate new clients is via paid advertisements, in either off-line or online media.

In other words, if you see others paying for advertising all the time, it's easy to begin believing that that's the way you can generate new business too.

But there is a substantial and fundamental difference between those who advertise a physical product and those who offer something that's intangible, or in the parlance of this book, someone who is Marketing The Invisible.

And I can sum up the difference with a simple analogy:

Marketing The Invisible is more like getting married than it is buying a car.

The difference is that, when you get married, you'd be wise to get to know the person very well before you either offer or accept a proposal.

With a car, though, you don't necessarily have to get to know the salesperson especially well, and you'll probably buy the car you really want, even if you don't like the salesperson.

That's because when you buy a car, you're not investing in a relationship; you're investing in a thing.

The difference is like night and day.

The number one mistake that I see amateur marketers making, time and again, is a failure to understand the critical importance of establishing a relationship of trust (at the very least) prior to bringing up the subject of working together.

I call it Premature Solicitation and, just like its premature counterpart in sex, it invariably ends up in frustration and disappointment for the other party.

When you get to Part Four, you'll be able to read how to create what I call "Psychological Allure," which takes the establishment of a trusted relationship to a depth that you probably never thought was possible.

There are four steps to the process of creating Psychological Allure, and each step leads your prospect to progressively deeper levels of being magnetically attracted to working with you.

The widespread mistake of believing that marketing is about a transaction, rather than a relationship, is manifested when professionals hire "appointment setters" to set up meetings with prospective clients. I've already hinted at why this mostly doesn't work, but I'll cover it in more depth again in the next chapter.

The same mistake is also evidenced when professionals buy a list and hope to generate quality clients from that list.

In Part Four, I not only outline the four steps for creating Psychological Allure, but I also go into detail about, and give specific examples of how to cultivate, that critical trust factor in the hearts and minds of people that you've never met, so that they can be moved from their naturally understandable and default position of skepticism, to a new mindset whereby you go beyond being their preferred choice of supplier to a place where you're seen as the *only* desirable supplier.

THE PROBLEM WITH THE MAJORITY OF MARKETING PROGRAMS AND COURSES

Most lead-generation methods that fail to bring in new clients are the result of two misconceptions.

Misconception number one is the idea that, if we can just find our ideal clients (buy a list, surf LinkedIn, or hire an agency to find people for us), then our marketing problems will be solved.

This is what I call the Find Them Mistake.

Misconception number two is equally faulty but has exactly the opposite idea — that we only need a way to have our ideal clients find us (sexy website, SEO, AdWords and so on), then our marketing problems will be solved.

This mistake is therefore called the Find Me Mistake.

By the end of this book, you will have been correctly indoctrinated in the understanding that finding the contact details of an ideal client, or finding a way to be sure that ideal client stumbles into your contact details, is about 10 percent of the ball game and, in fact, is the easiest part of the ball game.

The other 90 percent is leading that person (whether they found you or you found them) from a position of complete ignorance of who you are and what you do, to thinking that the idea of working with you is so desirous as to be compelling.

You have enormous potential to save yourself years of frustration and disappointment if you would take 60 seconds to contemplate those two common mistakes and recall them to mind anytime someone suggests a new website, SEO, online advertising, LinkedIn, social media marketing, or any the other methods that comprise the 10 percent of the ball game that I've mentioned above.

Understanding the Find Them and Find Me mistakes goes some way toward explaining why I must now confess to a deep and abiding frustration.

At times, my frustration verges on anger.

The source of these emotions comes from the many occasions when I've invested in training programs or courses with the goal of discovering strategies and tactics for growing my business.

Bear in mind that I'm in my fourth decade of starting and growing businesses, so I've had more opportunity than most to spend money on business improvement education.

I'm disappointed to report that on more than 90 percent of the occasions where I've invested significant money and bought into the promise of being given the keys to the business-growth kingdom, I've experienced no discernible improvement in my business results.

How about you?

When I ask Audiences to put their hands up if they feel that they wasted good money on training programs and courses that promised to show them how to bring new clients on board that simply didn't work, I always face a sea of raised hands.

This failure of the creators of these courses and programs to fulfill their promise can be attributed to them falling into one of two categories.

First, there are the charlatans.

The charlatans know what they are peddling doesn't work and they know that they are going to rip you off.

They are almost always effective marketers and their ability in that area is matched only by the unconscionable pleasure they experience when someone ill-advisedly buys from them. They are what I call Marketing Psychopaths.

Here is a list of psychopathic behavior from respected criminal psychologist Prof Robert Hare:

"Superficial charm, grandiose sense of self-worth, pathological lying, cunning/manipulative, lack of remorse, emotional shallowness, callousness and lack of empathy, unwillingness to accept responsibility for actions, a parasitic lifestyle, a lack of realistic long-term goals, impulsivity, irresponsibility."

That certainly describes some of the marketers that I've had the misfortune of meeting.

The second category are the Marketing Desperate.

These people mean well, but they are so far behind the eight ball financially that they cobble together anything they can, put a sexy looking cover on it (be that thing a book or a course or a program), and then go and flog it for all they're worth to cover up their cash-flow shortfall.

I'm not saying that I've always been the Mother Teresa of the marketing world, and I'll be the first to admit that there have been times over the last 40 years where I really needed that sale.

But I am saying that enough is enough, and that it would pay for you to be actively skeptical of anyone, including me, who makes the sort of promises that I'm making in this book.

So how can you sort out the good guys/girls from the bad guys/girls?

I'm going to cover that in Part Four when I outline The Four Steps of Investment Validation, which offers a virtually fail-proof formula for sorting out the Marketing Psychopaths and the Marketing Desperate from the people with the real oil, the stuff that actually works.

In the meantime, here's one clue: look for a money-back guarantee or, even better, a risk-reversal offer where you pay nothing until the seller has proven themselves trustworthy.

And please, don't just think of this in terms of people you may or may not be buying from.

There is far more benefit for you when you think about risk and trust from the perspective of your potential clients.

That's worth thinking about, and that's what we'll explore more in Part Four.

In the meantime, I'll sum up the problem of the traditional and commonly taught marketing methods by simply saying that the majority fail to deliver on their promise.

When I was learning to race super bikes, my instructor offered me the sage advice of: "Tom, if your balls are bigger than your brain, then you better get used to crashing... a lot."

On a similar note, if the Marketing Psychopaths and the Marketing Desperate possess a level of marketing ability that exceeds their value-delivery ability, then there's going to be a lot of crash and burning.

And unfortunately, it's going to be the buyers who suffer that fate.

That incredibly smart, creative, and generous man that goes by the name of Seth Godin (he is so famous that my dictation software knows how to type his name) titled one of his many books "All Marketers Are Liars."

Unfortunately, it turns out that he's not far from the truth.

Why You Should Avoid These 11 Commonly Taught Marketing Methods

IT'S EASY FOR me to sit here and write in general terms about why you have good reason to be skeptical of those who promote promises of wealth through marketing.

But it's not enough unless I back up my claims by giving you specific examples of marketing methods that are falsely touted as the answer to your lead-generation prayers.

So, without naming names, here is a list of commonly taught marketing methods that you should avoid, at the very least to begin with, including clear and specific reasons as to why you should steer clear of them.

I invite you to make up your own mind as to whether my reasons make good sense to you.

In reviewing this list and in considering my arguments, you will be potentially saving yourself the years of wasted time and money, and the years of frustration and disappointment that I experienced in figuring out that these methods should be avoided.

That's my gift to you, you can thank me when we meet.

But in the meantime, as you wisely and carefully read your way through this list, there's a chance that you may begin to feel depressed about the number of options for marketing that you thought you had, that I'm now blowing up to smithereens one by one.

If such a dark cloud appears to surface in your mind at any point during this next section, please pause and remind yourself that these few short minutes of pain are a worthy exchange for avoiding years of frustration and disappointment that would inevitably follow your experimenting with any of these forlorn methods.

I'm going to step on a lot of toes here because many of my contemporaries are recommending these methods. But I opened this book with the stated intention of telling you how it is, stripping out the hype and BS, and not holding back.

Before we launch into the list, I want to make it clear that I'm not saying that every single one of these commonly taught marketing methods is a dud. In fact, they fall into one of several categories:

1. There are methods that simply don't work at all.

2. There are methods that work moderately well but should be avoided because there are less-expensive and more-effective alternatives.

3. There are methods that won't generate leads, but are worth engaging in at some point in time to keep your brand in people's brains until they are ready to buy.

4. There are methods that are worth engaging in if you are a top-level marketer and have five figures a month to invest in lead generation.

Having said that, the common denominator for all 11 commonly recommended marketing methods is that you should avoid them, at the very least in the short term.

Here's my list and my reasons.

#1: POSTING ARTICLES ON LINKEDIN

The last time I checked with the queen of LinkedIn, Julie Mason, she told me that there were 7,222 articles posted to LinkedIn every single hour.

Of every day.

Of every week.

Of every year.

And that number will have been superseded by the time you read these words.

That's over 100 new articles every minute.

Your article is literally "gone in 60 seconds" and its burial process begins in an avalanche of other articles within a fraction of even that short period of time.

Even if one of my articles gets read, it's exceedingly unlikely that anyone is going to be so thunderstruck and awed by my genius that they'll pick up the phone or search for my "contact us" website page in the hope of becoming a client.

People (like me) who love to write articles are exceeded in their egocentricity only by narcissists, dictators, and cats (apologies to cat lovers, amongst whom I am one, but it's true).

Writers (again: guilty as charged) are in love with the idea that readers will be so moved by the profundity of what our stubby little fingers bang out on a keyboard that, given half a chance, they will toss rose petals before us wherever we walk.

The reality, however, is that most of the time, your biggest fan is actually you.

If you have any doubt that what I am saying is true, just try giving your latest dazzling article to your beloved husband/wife/partner to read, then sit back and pay careful attention to their eyes as they slowly glaze over and form a thick opaque appearance like the acting extras on the latest walking dead series live-streaming on Netflix.

That said, do I post to LinkedIn?

Absolutely.

But except for that blind squirrel thing (see above), I have zero expectation that anyone is going to become a client because of that posting.

So why do I do it?

Before I answer that, let me remind you that this section is all about why you should avoid certain commonly taught marketing methodologies if you want to develop effective lead generation.

And when I post to LinkedIn, I do so with zero expectation of generating a new client.

LinkedIn falls into the same category as many of the other marketing methodologies that you should avoid, because they are ineffective lead *generators*. But it is more than worthwhile to note that they can be very good lead *nurturers*.

And that's why I post to LinkedIn along with the Leadsology® Facebook Group, and it's why I tweet on Twitter and so on: to keep building my Brand in your Brain until you're ready to Buy (BBB).

I can write one article, or one blog post or one of whatever, and because I can re-purpose that same content across multiple platforms and to thousands of followers/subscribers/connections, it makes my efforts worthwhile.

With a relatively small investment of time and a little effort, I can establish and maintain credibility in the minds of those few whose attention I happen to attract by being in the right place at the right time.

In terms of lead generation, however, posting to LinkedIn is still a bit too random in terms of direct results for my liking. And if you're starting out in marketing, then it certainly should *not* be the first cab off your ranks.

There are more direct, more certain and more effective ways to generate leads in the short-to-medium term. We will get there in Part Three.

#2: ONLINE ADVERTISING AND FUNNELS

The Holy Grail of marketing is automation.

Millions of books, many online platforms and thousands of courses have been bought by seekers of that marketing Holy Grail.

Let's face it, the idea has incredibly strong appeal: sit on the beach with your laptop for 30 minutes a day, three days a week, and watch the millions roll in.

In terms of desirability, that concept pretty much hits the jackpot at 10 out of 10.

The only wee small tiny problem I have with this concept is that the majority of those offering advice on marketing automation (by no means all of them) are promoting methods that either don't work or significantly understate the amount of work or time involved to make it all effective.

ONLINE FUNNELS ARE COMPLICATED

The reality of online advertising and online funnels is that they have a lot of moving parts, and they take a lot of time and effort to construct in a way that delivers a return on investment.

Actually, I have no problem with that.

I'm into what works; whether that's a complicated thing or a simple thing, whether it's harder or easier, my main question is "does this thing actually generate results?"

The unpalatable fact for many remains that setting these things up requires split-testing, and that split-testing is not a one-off proposition: it's ongoing and constant.

For example, you need to run two Facebook advertisements simultaneously and figure out which one is getting the most clicks.

Split-testing means that, once you have a champion advertisement, you then kill off the loser and replace it with another challenger.

And as mentioned, this is an ongoing process: the creation of a new advertisement, the commitment of a fresh budget, meticulous daily tracking and measuring of results in a timely and accurate manner.

Find another champion, kill the loser, rinse and repeat.

It's a treadmill.

And it never ends.

Not only do you need to repeat that process with the advertisement, you also need to repeat it with two landing pages, find a landing page champion, kill off the loser, track and measure the results, rinse and repeat.

That's because you've not only got to measure which Facebook advertisement is attracting the most clicks, you must work out which landing page is generating the most subscriber opt-ins.

And the thing that you're offering on that landing page (your honey pot), be it a Special Report, a series of short training videos, a downloadable checklist, a diagnostic tool, a survey... or whatever, they also must be continually killed off and recreated.

That's because, embedded in your honey pot will be your call to action, and that needs to be split-tested along with everything else.

One call to action might be for the Audience to invest in a low-cost course, whereas another might be to book a time to speak with you about becoming a client. Which one is most effective for generating new clients and revenue? That's what split-testing, tracking, and measuring will determine.

In short, if you want to run online advertisements and online funnels, it's a bucket load of work and sitting on a beach for 30 minutes a day with your laptop and expecting money to wash over your beautiful sunbaked body ain't gonna happen.

ONLINE ADVERTISING WITH ONLINE FUNNELS IS EXPENSIVE

In addition to online advertising and online funnels being complicated and requiring your serious and constant attention, they have also become quite expensive lead generators.

And when I say, "lead generators," that is really an exaggeration.

What they actually are is "opt-in generators," and they produce what I'd call "suspects" as opposed to prospects.

Anyhow, back to the fact that online advertisements have become expensive.

10 years ago, I could generate a suspect/opt-in for around two dollars a shot.

That's steadily climbed to over $10 per successful opt-in as more and more people jump on board the online funnel bandwagon.

And putting modesty aside just for a moment (I hope you realize how privileged you are to be witnessing this rare event!), I have some idea of what I'm doing when it comes to marketing because I've been doing this for the thick end of 40 years.

And while we're on the subject of money, a common mistake among newbies to the world of online advertising is that they can start with a budget of maybe $10 a day, test and measure the results, and then throw more money at it once the conversions are working well.

The problem with that idea can be explained with the concept of "Statistical Significance" and I'll explain what I mean by that with a brief story.

Way back in 1997, after I had launched a business that went on to become successful internationally, I had the opportunity to have a private chat with Chris Newton, who to this day remains, in my humble opinion, a truly remarkable marketer.

Bear in mind that way back in the dark ages of 1997, the Internet was still in its commercial infancy.

Yes, there were websites and yes, we had email but no, there was no such thing as internet marketing and there was no such thing as webinars or downloadable guides or online surveys and Facebook didn't exist and neither did LinkedIn and **www.amazon.com** featured a whopping five products.

All of which I mention just to remind you that, outside of mainstream media advertising (radio, television, newspapers), the closest thing we marketers had to an affordable and effective marketing medium was physical direct postal mail.

To promote my business, I'd book a conference venue, buy a list of business owners along with their postal addresses, and then I'd send out 3,000 letters inviting those business owners to attend a free seminar (which was a bit like inviting a fly to join a spider at the center of his web).

I'd have my wife and kids and whoever else was unlucky enough to be hovering around the office at the time, fold thousands of letters and stuff them into thousands of envelopes and stick thousands of stamps onto the aforementioned envelopes.

What this added up with was at least a $5,000 investment into every monthly campaign.

If it fizzed, it hurt like hell. So, I was determined to maximize every dollar spent on my marketing.

At the time, I was fortunate enough to have a friend who kindly introduced me, at a cost of $4,000, to a marketing consultant who gave me some advice and then sold me a $10,000 marketing course that was created by Chris Newton. Talk about up-selling.

I'm not sure if I ever truly thanked Kevin for extracting that $14,000 out of my bank account, so here we go: thank you Kevin.

It was in fact an excellent investment, even though it hurt like hell at the time.

Having read almost every word that Chris Newton had written up until that point, I was something of a Newton Groupie. So, when the chance came during an overseas trip to spend 15 minutes alone with him in his office, I seized on the opportunity to ask him about my marketing campaigns and how I could improve them.

As he always is, Chris was as gracious as he was articulate and helpful.

He introduced me to the concept of Statistical Significance, meaning that to draw reliable conclusions from the results of any marketing campaign, one had to send enough direct mailers.

When I asked Chris what that number was, he replied "30,000." And he added that was just one side of the split-test.

In other words, to arrive at conclusions which were reliable enough on which to base a decision as to which direct mail piece was more effective, I had to split-test between two campaigns and a total of 60,000 mail pieces which would have been a cost of some $72,000.

I simply didn't have the budget for that, so I kept plodding along, somewhat successfully, with a smaller number of direct mail pieces each month until I discovered the concept of Other Peoples Networks (OPN), at which point in time my marketing budget was cut to zero without my results suffering even a minor dent (more on OPN in Part Three).

Which brings me nicely back to my main point, which is that $10 a day on Facebook advertisements is not going to get you anywhere near Statistical Significance. Instead, it will have you running around in circles day after day watching your money quietly disappear into Mark Zuckerberg's coffers at a small but horrifyingly steady rate.

Case in point… Once my Facebook advertisements started to cost me $12 per opt-in, I got out of them.

It's not that I was losing money at $12 per opt-in, it was just that they became very expensive, relative to other options.

I can understand why people fall in love with the idea of online advertisements, but they soon fall out of love with them when they find out to create a flow of free subscribers using OPN.

In Part Three, I'll reveal how I increased my list by 864 semi-qualified subscribers for zero dollars with just one OPN exercise, and I'll further reveal how you can grow your list virtually every single day of the year without paying even one cent to anyone at any time for anything.

If, therefore, you can get semi-qualified opt-ins to your list for free, and you can automate those opt-ins so they happen even while you're asleep or on holiday, why the heck would anyone want to blow their budget on online advertising?

At the current rate of $12 per opt-in using Facebook advertisements, the 864 subscribers I mentioned above would have cost me $10,368. With OPN, they were free, and I regard that as a much better price.

In summary, the complexity and cost of online advertisements are why you should avoid them and look at alternative generation options, such as the ones identified in the next part of this book.

#3: HIRING APPOINTMENT-SETTERS

The concept of appointment-setters is terrific.

You hand over $500 and the appointment-setting agency hooks you up with 10 appointments with people who allegedly have an interest in working with you.

What's not to like about this concept?

You get to do what you do best, which is to talk to people who have an interest in becoming a client, and then to work with those new clients.

None of that messy and awkward marketing stuff.

Great idea, right?

Unfortunately, wrong!

Appointment-setters often consist of a team of people sitting in an office situated in a country where labor costs are lower. Each team member is assigned a client, such as you, to generate appointments for. They search the Internet (typically LinkedIn) for the people who have a profile matching that of your ideal client.

They connect with those target individuals and ask them directly if they have a need for the services you offer.

Those who respond positively are invited to make a time to talk with you, typically on a Skype call or similar.

Personally, I have zero problem with some of the ideas incorporated into this concept.

For example, it makes good sense to outsource some of the work to low-cost regions, because it will free up your time and it's relatively inexpensive, plus it provides work for people who might otherwise struggle to earn a decent living.

Apart from one teensy-weensy detail, everyone's winning.

That annoying little detail unfortunately has to do with the results, which are either of poor quality or non-existent.

Most of the targeted people will not respond with any interest to the approach of an appointment set.

But that's not your problem.

At this stage, your brand has not even been mentioned and appointment-setters have a well-deserved reputation for endless patience. They know how to play the numbers game.

Of the very small percentage that book a time to speak with you, less than half will show up to the meeting.

That fact on its own is not really a big problem because if you had say, 10 people who didn't show up but drew another 10 quality appointments each month with people eager to work with you, I'd imagine you be quite happy with that net outcome.

The trouble is though, of the ones who do show up to a meeting, virtually all of them will be broke.

But hey, even if one person a month showed up, had the money to pay you what you charge, and had a genuine interest in the type of service you offer, you'd be right in thinking that would make the whole deal worthwhile.

The problem is that one person will want to "think it over."

Translated, that means they are not convinced that you are their best option and they'll want to explore alternatives prior to making any commitment.

Extrapolated, that means they'll ride off into the sunset, fully intending to check out all their options and then they'll become distracted with the daily items that consume their attention and which present a more pressing priority than undertaking due diligence on you and your competitors.

The bottom line is that regardless of whatever assurances these people give you, and regardless of whatever promises they make, and regardless of whatever their real intentions may be, you and your wonderful service WILL drop off the radar scope of their mind, if not within a few days, then within a few hours.

Appointment-setters can work, but mostly for people offering physical products or for those who offer very low-cost services.

But I'm willing to bet that what you offer you doesn't fit into either of those categories (a physical product or a cheap service), which is why I'm recommending that you avoid appointment-setters and instead adopt the recommendations I outline in Part Three.

Before we finish this little section, let me reveal why, apart from the above-mentioned exceptions, appointment-setting is very unlikely to work well for you.

The reason can be found in the Preface, where I explain that Marketing The Invisible is more like getting married than it is buying a car.

For people to hand over a significant amount of money, you need to develop a high level of trust, and they need to be convinced not only about your professional integrity, but about how well your service will meet their exact needs.

You may be able to achieve the latter during the first meeting with the prospect, but to achieve the former you are going to need to have one or two more honey pots for them to sample — see my analogy above about Bears and honey pots.

(BTW: they also need to be convinced that they'll implement what you give them, but that's another story that we'll deal with in Part Four under the subject of The Four Investment Validations that prospects seek when attempting to determine if they should invest with you.)

Just a reminder that, while it may seem a little negative for me to be kicking off a book on marketing with all the things that you should *not* do, allow me to invoke the ghost of Mark Twain and remind you that…

> "It's not the things that we don't know that hurt us,
>
> it's the things we think we know that just ain't so."

When it comes to marketing, never were truer words spoken.

#4: Spending Money on Mainstream Media Advertising

I won't spend much time on this one because most professionals no longer seriously consider taking out advertisements on a radio or television show or in their national/state newspaper.

But as a professional marketer way back in 1997, I figured I had to try every medium so I could legitimately validate whether they would work for my clients or not.

That cost me a lot of money!

And as mentioned, I found it incredibly difficult to advise my clients against spending money on, say, radio advertising, until I verified whether it was possible to enjoy a return on investment from that medium.

I was never able to generate a return on investment from mainstream newspaper advertisements and it was even quite difficult to do so from the journals of carefully targeted associations.

I was however sometimes able to at least break even with radio advertisements provided we targeted only rush-hour traffic times.

But with so many other alternatives that required little or no financial outlay, it simply didn't make sense to persist with paid advertising.

There is one exception to my recommendation of avoiding paid advertising.

That exception is a carefully created advertisement in a local newspaper that offers the type of professional service or advice which the public considers to be a commodity or "package" that offers the prospect of a fast solution to those who have a high awareness of their need.

For example, I've worked with several family lawyers (AKA divorce attorneys) and we've successfully generated a regular flow of high-quality leads by promoting an initial consultation with the promise of several key recommendations that would help the client make the journey of getting through their divorce and transitioning to their new life a whole lot smoother and faster.

But that's the rare exception and even then, that medium should never be used as a complete marketing system, but rather as one stream of leads to be complemented with others. Overall, such advertising is ineffective, other than for creating and sustaining brand awareness, for services to clients who are not motivated by a sense of urgency: e.g. consultancy and other advisory services.

#5: Public Relations and Press Releases

This one falls into the blind squirrel category and for the sake of simplicity, I'm going to include media interviews such as radio, morning television, or newspapers/magazines.

If you're clever enough to create a press release and actually have a media outlet publish it, then it's great credibility for you, and the fact that your ideas have been published can be included on your website and in your bio.

But don't expect your phone to ring loudly or long with a queue of people wanting to work with you.

In short, PR is worthwhile as a brand awareness builder provided you are not pumping any significant amounts of money into it.

And while you're on the subject of "as seen on," when you see the logos of CBS News, ABC, NBC, and Fox on someone's website, you should know that it's more than likely that the permission to use those logos has been purchased from a brand broker and not actually secured by personal appearances on those mediums.

This can quite rightly be called "fake news." Sad, but true.

You have been warned.

While it may be legal to purchase permission to use the logos of media outlets such as the above, I'd personally be quite dubious about the integrity of the service I was about to invest in, since the owner of that service is comfortable with leading me to believe a thing that simply wasn't true, i.e. that they were guests on some of the biggest media outlets in the world

Potentially damaging admission: I was recently approached and asked to pay $1,200 for the right to use the above logos on my website and in other promotional material.

It was a client of mine who approached me about the idea, and I have a lot of respect for him professionally and personally. But at the end of the day, I couldn't arrive at a level of comfort around the idea, simply because it was disingenuous, non-authentic and, in my heart of hearts, I knew it was just downright misleading.

(The ironic thing is that I've actually appeared on CBS, and to my chagrin I have still not milked that particular cow like I should have.)

Most PR campaigns produce a lot of metaphorical froth and bubble which may be very exciting at the time. But just like the literal counterparts, they tend to fall flat all too quickly and leave you with a rather flat bank account.

#6: TRADE SHOWS

Trade shows can be terrific sales generators if you have a specialty physical product.

For example, if you're selling a super-yacht with gold plated toilet seats and seven helicopter pads then the right trade show may help you to ship a few units (pardon the pun).

But if you are a consultant or a corporate trainer or you are a coach offering specialized services, then setting up your booth is the equivalent of putting up a large banner which loudly proclaims to your prospective clients that you are most definitely not in demand.

That wouldn't be a problem, except for the fact that as human beings we are wired to demonstrate far less interest in those things that we know we can have at any time.

It's part of our evolutionary survival system.

We are programmed to experience an increase in desire and motivation when a thing is scarce (such as food, water or shelter) and to conversely experience apathy when a thing is openly available.

What I'm suggesting may be validated and verified by the countless number of effective marketing campaigns out there, including those horrible infomercials that we all hate (but that many of us buy from) where the price offered, or a bonus, is available only for a brief period of time or for the first X number of buyers.

Witness also a couple dating for the first time. Let's call them Sam and Pam.

If Sam instantly falls in love with Pam on the very first date and fails to hold himself back, but instead is in Pam's face physically and holding her hand in a vice-like grip and declaring his undying love and his unshakable desire to spend every last second of the next 50 years by her side, there's a very strong chance that there will be no second date.

And that's the fundamental problem in engaging with a trade show.

You're firstly positioning yourself as being readily available (resulting in unconscious apathy from your Audience) and even worse, you'll be perceived as being in a state of need, like poor Sam above, and that's a killer punch sequence which will drive your prospective clients into the arms of your competitors.

And once again, even if our friend the blind squirrel popped up again from time to time during the trade show, you should avoid the temptation to book a booth because there are more effective and cost-free ways to generate new client inquiries (see Part Three).

#7: Business Networking Meetings

I'm a great admirer of Dr. Ivan Misner and, like Seth Godin, he's so famous that even my dictation software knows who he is.

In case his ubiquitous presence has somehow escaped your attention, Ivan is the founder of Business Network International, or BNI as it is more commonly known.

As such, he is both the founder and highly-esteemed leader of one of the world's largest franchise organizations.

And he was kind enough to give me a rather flattering review for my last best-selling book, which makes me even more inclined to sing his praises.

That aside, you don't get to claim a membership of 227,000 across 8,211 chapters worldwide, generating an estimated $9.3 billion annually in referral business, without something working spectacularly well.

So, having witnessed the good doctor generate such extraordinary success, why on earth would I have business networking meetings on my top 11 list of marketing methodologies to avoid, at least in the short term?

There are two primary reasons, one of which you should ignore completely unless you can relate to it, and the other to which you should play careful attention.

The first reason is that like many writers, I'm a hermit.

When I'm sitting in my office in our house, which in turn is sitting on the sand next to the beach, and I can hear my best friend, Monty The Marketing Wonder Dog, quietly snoring next to me, I feel like the luckiest man in the world.

In short, I am comfortable in my own skin and I am exceptionally socially retarded.

So, the idea of dressing up (I'm currently sitting here in my board shorts and a white T-shirt with bare feet, unshaven and with no underpants – sorry, probably more information than you needed) and getting in my car (which I hate cleaning because there are more interesting things to do) and traveling to a meeting where strange people will want to smile and shake hands with me (horror of horrors) while I sip bad coffee and make small talk, is not something I like to do.

I've always been like that, but in addition…

15 months ago, I had an adventure in the world of brain hemorrhages.

One of these little suckers kills 50 percent of people my age and permanently brain-damages another 41 percent.

I had three of them.

When my wife came to visit me after the operation, which was precipitated by the third hemorrhage, she asked me how it all went.

The fact that I wasn't in a straitjacket, gnashing my teeth and frothing at the mouth was probably a clue that things had gone okay.

"Pretty well actually," I said. "The surgeon explained that there is only a small amount of permanent damage and that's contained within the motor neuron section of my brain... in the part that knows how to wash dishes. So that option is sadly no longer available."

"And," I added, "I can't be positive, but I'm pretty sure that the neurons that know how to do vacuum cleaning are completely shot as well."

Strangely, she didn't believe me.

However, that's a true story and the point of relating it to you is that, since my little adventure with bleeding brains, I resolved that those things that I don't want to do, that I don't like to do, that I don't have to do, I am not going to do anymore.

The list of things that I ain't gonna do anymore includes weeding, gardening, getting up on the roof to clean out the guttering, washing cars, running large product launches, running large conference events, and working with people who are even more weird than I am (there has to be a limit to the amount of weirdness I allow in my life and I suspect that I max that limit our pretty well on my own). But at the very top of that list is business networking.

So, if you're like me and you don't enjoy going to business networking meetings, then (Dr. Ivan please forgive me), don't do them.

If, however, you really enjoy going to those meetings, then I'll be the first one to encourage you to do so, because while facts can mislead, in the case of BNI, they don't lie, and you may well indeed pick up a client through business networking meetings.

I said there was a second reason and so, with the caveat of the last paragraph, here it is: I encourage a large majority of my clients to develop scalable value delivery.

That means that, in most cases, I want them to have the capacity to deliver value beyond the reach of their state or national borders.

Now, before you reject this idea by telling yourself that you must be in-person with a client to deliver value, let me assure you that in 90 percent of the cases that I've worked with, that's simply not true.

It may be true for a portion of the work that you do, but once you create a segmented list of exactly how clients gain value from your services, I'll bet you dollars to donuts that is a fair chunk of value which you can deliver virtually.

That's all I'll say on the subject at this point, but my second book *The Million Dollar Ceiling*, would help your thinking in this regard as will Part Six, where I cover the subject of scalability.

In the meantime, it stands to reason that if you can scale your value delivery beyond your local borders, then you should be maximizing that opportunity by scaling your lead generation as well.

And for all the merits of business networking meetings, scalability is not one of them.

#8: PHYSICAL MARKETING EVENTS

Marketing your services by holding a public seminar, workshop, or conference is without doubt one of the best ways to produce a high number of high-quality new client inquiries.

But they are a heck of a lot of work and they can also consume a fair chunk of money.

The reason that physical events work so well as lead generators is that they provide you with the time and space you need to build your credibility in the minds of your Audience.

And that credibility is built faster when you are in front of your Audience as a three-dimensional being, rather than being beamed through a webinar or a livestream on Facebook.

In short, nothing is as good as being there.

I've run literally hundreds of physical marketing events across multiple countries and generated millions of dollars for various businesses in the process.

So, this particular item on my list of traditional marketing methodologies to avoid falls into the category of: "by all means have a crack at this thing, but don't make it one of the first things you try."

That's not only because of the complexity of successfully running such events, but also because of the time and money they eat up and the fact that, if you're going to invest that sort of resource into an event, you better try and generate new leads with a lower cost medium such as webinars or other online meetings.

Once you've proven that your marketing message is compelling enough for people to register and attend an online event, and you've proven that your presentation will convert enough people into inquiries, and you've proven that you can convert those inquiries into clients, then — and only then — should you venture into the costlier world of running physical events.

By the way, in Part Four, I'll walk you through my 10-part Leadsology® Persuasion Sequence which you will be able to swipe and deploy for all your presentations, both off-line and online, so that you maximize the number of leads generated from each event.

#9: Product Launches

A product launch typically involves a carefully planned and scheduled sequence of events with a goal of making a lot of sales over a relatively short period time.

The most successful product launches will take months, if not a year or more, to prepare for.

Very often, a launch involves dozens if not hundreds of affiliates, each with their own email list, who send out promotional emails that have been prepared by the Seller.

The core idea behind a launch is that you pick a specific date and time to announce to the world that the course, or whatever it is that is being sold, is available for purchase, but only for a limited number of days.

Naturally there are bonuses and discounts on offer, for that limited period of time.

Often there is a pre-launch phase which builds up the tension for prospective buyers and this can involve lots of honey pots, including surveys, quizzes, webinars, and so on.

If you've ever been on the receiving end of a product launch that's been well executed, it's really quite impressive.

The big launches will pull in millions of dollars in revenue and many of the members of the mastermind group that I'm involved with have completed successful launches.

What you don't see is everything that goes on behind the scenes.

One of the recently completed a million-dollar launches sounds very impressive until you realize that the affiliate commissions, contractors' fees and costs of various software platforms totaled $800,000.

And when you throw into the equation that it took 12 months of hard work to plan that product launch, then you've got you ask yourself if there aren't easier ways to generate $200,000, which was his net profit.

In summary, product launches are on this list of traditionally taught marketing methods that you should avoid, because to do them well requires a long-term effort, and the ability to manage a complex network of relationships as well as being very clever in containing costs.

Product launches are a bit like physical marketing events: there are easier, simpler, less expensive and less stressful ways to generate new clients.

#10: BLOGGING AND PODCASTING

If you want to generate new client inquiries from blogging and/or podcasting, then you'll be pleased to know that it's very simple.

All you must do is produce a blog or podcast of high quality, at least once a week, for the next five years, and then the leads will start to flow.

That may sound a little cynical, but it's not too wide of the mark.

And if you're not prepared to commit and deliver on the regularity of production that's required to establish a reputation of reliability and value, then you're better off not starting at all.

There are a few things that will destroy your credibility faster than a series of blog posts, totaling five, with the last one posted 18 months ago. Not a good look.

So, should you blog or podcast?

Absolutely!

At Leadsology®, our goal is to produce our video blog (VLOG) as both a video and a podcast 40 times per year.

But just quietly, between you and me, I still don't expect it to generate many, if any, new client inquiries.

Social media posting such as blogs and podcasts are best produced with the objective of keeping your Brand in your market's Brain until they are ready to Buy (BBB).

And as such, they are well worth publishing, especially if you take my approach, which is to do as little as possible to achieve the purpose of the blog or podcast.

Think about that.

If your purpose is BBB, then you don't need to spend a lot of time to achieve that.

In point of fact, one of the greatest and most sought-after speakers on the subject of marketing is Seth Godin who produces blogs of three or four sentences. Pithy pearls of wisdom.

So, there's no need to spend an hour a day typing up your blog masterpiece when five minutes will achieve the purpose just as well.

Similarly, I've switched many clients off the idea of producing a monthly newsletter (tedious and time-consuming to produce and boring to read) and instead replaced that with a simple inspirational "quote of the week" which can be distributed through the email list and social media along with their brand.

That way, our objective of BBB is achieved faster and simpler and with a fraction of the time and effort.

The same principle applies to everything else you do in marketing: consider the purpose of what you want to achieve prior to creating the Asset which you hope will achieve that purpose.

And choose an Asset which achieves that purpose with as little fuss and bother as possible.

A thing (a presentation, a blog, an email, a landing page, a webinar, a book, and so on) should be as long as it takes to get the goal achieved, and then as short as possible.

#11: SOCIAL MEDIA SITES SUCH AS FACEBOOK, TWITTER, INSTAGRAM AND PINTEREST

I've already dropped several hints as to what I regard the purpose of social media to be, which can be summed up with the three Bs: to keep your Brand in their Brain until they are ready to Buy (BBB).

Most of our postings to various social media sites simply repurpose material from existing content.

For example: the Marketing The Invisible (MTI) VLOG and podcast is distributed via email to our subscribers as well as being posted to Facebook, Twitter, and LinkedIn at a minimum.

MTI runs for exactly seven minutes and takes not much more of my time personally to produce than that seven minutes.

With the click of a few buttons, my erstwhile assistant spreads the good news that the latest episode has been released via our email list and all the main social media platforms.

But remember that posting to social media sites is like blogging or podcasting: it's a slow burn.

Therefore, once again, I recommend that you put the idea of social media on your mental shelf to start with, and come back and revisit it once you've developed lead systems that deliver results faster and in a more direct manner.

What I mean by the latter comment is that social media is not the best medium through which to pitch the offer of booking a time to talk with you. People who go to social media sites are primarily motivated to seek out engaging content and to be entertained, as opposed to being pitched to.

Contrast that to people who attend your breakfast presentation, or your webinar, or your boardroom briefing, or your seminar (and so on), who are primarily motivated by the thought of learning and professional development.

In that context, it is reasonable to assume that the presenter (you) will offer further opportunities for learning and professional development, and the most logical step in that direction would be to book a time to speak with you about whether what you have is a fit for their needs.

Whew.

At this stage, I'm breathing a quiet and gentle side of relief.

That's because now that I've gotten the "don't do this stuff" out of the way, I can introduce you to the more positive side of this book, which is to outline the lead generation methods that bring in predictable and repeatable results.

Hallelujah — let's kick into it.

PART TWO

SETTING A STRONG FOUNDATION FOR LEAD GENERATION BY GAINING A STRATEGIC UNDERSTANDING OF MARKETING THE INVISIBLE

Introduction to Marketing Strategy

I **WANT TO ASK** you to invest just a little time to gain a rudimentary but important understanding of inbound marketing strategy.

The reason that this is important is that most people (around 95 percent) make the major mistake of rushing into the tactical side of marketing, such as placing an advertisement or writing a book or promoting a webinar or hiring a digital agency, without having taken the time to answer the four critical strategic questions that I am about to reveal to you.

But first let me give you a workable definition of what I mean by inbound marketing strategy.

In the context of this book, I can define inbound marketing as being the thing that generates a weekly, if not daily, flow of highly qualified prospective clients, contacting you to find out more about working with you.

And those prospective clients will already have a pretty good idea of your fee size and how you work with clients.

There probably are well over 1,000 definitions of marketing, but anything that produces a result like that, I am more than happy to put my name to and call inbound marketing.

Strategy is a little trickier to define but in order to gain clarity on the concept, please allow me to first tell you what it's not.

Strategy is not tactics, the latter being the execution of your marketing. Running a webinar is a tactic. Publishing a book is a tactic. Organizing a marketing event or a seminar are both tactics.

Strategy, on the other hand, identifies who your ideal client is, and what their specific unmet need is, as well as understanding their values/needs/motivations in the context of your industry segment.

Strategy also articulates what your target Audience needs to see or hear in order to gain their attention and motivate them to want to take the next step, and it also identifies the most effective mediums for getting that Message out to that Audience.

Don't bother underlining anything from the above two paragraphs because I'll break it down for you, step-by-step, right now.

Another way of explaining strategy is that it's all about creating competitive advantage, as well as planning how that will be executed.

As soon as you start building and deploying the Assets to execute your strategy, you've moved into the realm of tactics.

I mentioned that in my previous book *Leadsology®: The Science of Being In Demand*. I laid out a 10-part strategic model for marketing services, advice, or software.

In the Preface, I also mentioned that the book that you're now reading will drill down and look at the first four parts of that model in more detail than my last book.

So that's what we're going to do right now.

In my previous book, those first four parts were identified as:

1. Magic

2. Market

3. Message

4. Mediums

So that I can be more accurate and detailed about each part, I'm going to switch things up a little bit in this book and change the names of those parts to the following:

1. Magic

2. Audience (previously referred to as Market)

3. Message

4. Assets (previously referred to as Mediums)

So, if you've read my previous book, that little explanation should keep you safely away from the edges of the cliffs of confusion.

Lastly, before we dive into the chapter, I want to let you know that I'll be presenting each of those four parts in the form of a question designed to help you come up with the answer for your service, advice, or software-based business.

The Magic

STRATEGIC QUESTION #1: WHAT'S THE MAGIC YOU'LL BE MARKETING?

JUST THIS MORNING, I referred a potential client to my free lead gen challenge at **www.fivehourchallenge.com** because I wasn't convinced that he had some Magic.

I'd have loved to be able to make his wallet a little lighter and enrolled him in one of my programs, but the reality is that without something which is both transformational and differentiated, it is really hard to create effective lead generation systems.

Contrast that with Frank, my software-genius client in Philadelphia, who supplies organizations with contractors who possess specialized skills in areas such as machine learning and big data.

One of the big problems with leading-edge software development is the non-completion rate for those projects and, even worse, the low rate of usage by the intended end-users.

For years, Frank's organization has delivered a 100 percent completion rate and, as far as can be humanly measured, a near 100 percent implementation level for end-users.

And thereby, Frank hits twin bull's-eyes for both offering something which is transformational and differentiated from his competitors.

That's a much easier value proposition to successfully market than someone who's offering Microsoft Excel spreadsheet training.

It's the Magic that makes the marketing potent.

In my world, no Magic equals no marketing.

Having laid down that foundation principle, let's return to the question of what's the Magic you'll be marketing?

You may think that you know the answer to this question, but once again there is a possibility that what you think you know is hurting you.

Allow me to explain.

A recent Canadian client of mine, Susan, had a wonderful website which listed exactly 14 of her specialties, which included 360-degree feedback, leadership development, organizational change, strategic planning, and human dynamics, whatever that is.

At the very first meeting, we explored each of those specialties and I grew increasingly confident that she was indeed very capable in each of those 14 areas.

The meeting with Susan was online and we both had our webcams on, so I could clearly see her face when, having talked about all the things she was offering, I quietly spoke two simple words: "pick one."

Susan's face suddenly resembled that of a deer paralyzed in the headlights of an oncoming vehicle.

After a few seconds, she regained her composure, looked at me with still wide eyes and asked: "what do you mean?"

I told her that I needed her to pick one specialty that we would focus on marketing.

Strategy implies focus. And you can't focus on marketing three things initially and simultaneously, let alone 14 things.

And there's a fair chance that you're like Susan, in that you have many specialties that you've developed over many years and that, again like Susan, you can deliver significant value in each and every area.

So pick one.

And everything else is to come off your website, off your business card, off your LinkedIn profile, off your landing pages and off anything else that a potential ideal client could read and readily discover online or off-line, about what it is that you do.

This concept may come as a shock to you, like it was for Susan, but I can assure you that it is a prerequisite to maximizing the impact of your marketing.

Whether or not, like Susan, you can genuinely deliver value across multiple disciplines, most of your potential new ideal clients won't believe that you can.

Given that most people won't believe that you are a specialist in multiple areas, their default belief becomes that you must be a general practitioner.

And you only need to cast your eyes to the medical fraternity to confirm the fact that specialists are invariably more in demand than general practitioners and that because of that increased demand, they command much higher fees.

In summary, you need to feature and actively market only one thing from all the things you can do because firstly, it's impossible to effectively market multiple specialties both initially and simultaneously, and secondly because you'll become a more highly desirable supplier and able to command a premium due to the fact that you're perceived to be a specialist who is in great demand.

So, the question therefore becomes, which segment of your Magic do you pick?

And I'll answer that question with a series of other questions which go like this...

Of all the things you can offer to the market, which segment...

Q1: ...is the most profitable?

Q2: ...do you enjoy the most?

Q3: ...can you deliver a significant and measurable transformation in?

Q4: ...is in demand by a market that you can reach with your message?

Q5: ...is the one that is easiest to generate interest in?

Q6: …is the one that has relatively less competition?

Q7: …is the one for which you can most easily scale value delivery?

The easiest way to figure this out is to list your various specialties and give each specialty a tick for every question above that you can answer with a yes.

The specialty with the most ticks becomes the Magic that you'll be marketing.

And of course, if you don't like the answer, then you should feel at liberty to pick the second most highly rated segment, or the third.

So long as you pick a segment that definitely scores ticks for the first four questions at a minimum.

By way of further example, I have close to 40 years of marketing and management experience and, as you would hope, I've learned a thing or two in that time.

I'm confident and capable of helping clients with any number of leadership, sales, management, and marketing disciplines, including strategic planning, successor planning, hiring and selection, KPI dashboards, performance appraisal, and a whole bunch more.

But I figured out many years ago that the "low-lying fruit" and the specialty that scored seven out of a potential seven ticks, was lead generation.

To that end, you won't find anything else other than lead generation on my website, on my LinkedIn profile, or on my business card, should I be bothered to get one.

What I'm talking about here is sometimes referred to as your "front end."

That term can have many meanings, but it's pertinent and relevant for the concept of picking one specialty/segment to market. Once you have a client on board and they are overjoyed at the value you are delivering, you can at that point introduce them to your other specialties.

But you have a snowball's chance in hell of marketing multiple specialties, initially and simultaneously, so I beg of you: pick one!

At this point, it's worth repeating the seven ways of increasing the desirability of your value proposition in your marketplace.

I covered this concept under the title "The Value Slider" in my previous book, but it was so popular that it's worth repeating here. It's worth repeating also because it may give you useful food for thought when choosing the segment that you'll be marketing.

Here are the several ways that you can increase desirability for your value proposition:

1. Offer a measurable transformation.

2. Offer a significantly greater transformation.

3. Offer a transformation that you can deliver faster.

4. Offer a better return on investment (not cheaper!).

5. Offer a transformation that's simpler to implement.

6. Offer a transformation that you make easier to achieve.

7. Offer a transformation that's more relevant to the client's needs.

Remember: before you do any marketing whatsoever, pick one!

Then figure out how to successfully generate leads for that one segment.

When you're successfully generating leads and you're successfully converting those leads into clients and you're successfully delivering value to those clients, then, and only then, you can choose whether you want to switch to another segment or add another segment.

There's an old builder's adage which says, "measure twice and cut once."

Picking one is a big decision. Do it carefully so you don't have to "cut twice."

But having done that, then stick to the task of perfecting your lead-generation systems until you get them working incredibly well, and don't add new segments or switch to another segment until you've got that beachhead established.

The reason I'm banging on about this is that all too often I see people picking a segment and then failing to persist through the inevitable hard yards needed to break through the obstacles on the road that leads to successful marketing.

Too many people are looking for the magic bullet, the one thing, the simple formula.

It doesn't exist.

Even when my clients work with me, and even though I train them well and give them proven, step-by-step templates, guides and action items, they still must persist through obstacles. They still have to think and observe and take corrective action and refine where and when it makes sense. That's just the way it works.

Never make the mistake of thinking I, or anyone else, is some form of savior who is going to take all the pain and effort away without you doing some of the work — and far more importantly, contributing to the thinking process.

When I work with new clients, I invariably explain to them that this will be like a dance. They'll bring their knowledge of their services and marketplace to the dance and I'll bring my knowledge of marketing.

But to make the thing work, we both must dance. Dancing looks pretty freakin' weird when just one of us is dancing and the other is watching.

To sum up, pick one, but step up and accept that you are the one who ultimately is going to have to think and choose which one to pick.

Never delegate your authority for such decisions to any teacher, trainer or even a globally acclaimed marketing guru.

Of the few people who really know what they are talking about in terms of Marketing The Invisible, none of them should take the place of your own mind.

What we are here for is to eliminate virtually all the mistakes that you can make and save you years of disappointment and frustration in trying to figure this thing out for yourself.

We can also massively accelerate your progress toward your goal, but we should never be seen as the repository of all wisdom and knowledge.

Like everything else in life, it comes down to a balance. When you work with a mentor, and there's too much of the mentor, then you fall well short of your potential.

And when you work with a mentor, and there is too much of you… Guess what?

Yep, you fall well short of your potential.

On a final note, I'd like to comment on the subject of passion.

A lot of people talk about how passionate they are about what they do.

Unfortunately, in the commercial world, most people wouldn't give a rat's whatever for what someone is passionate about.

It's nice if they love what they do, but if that's the case, and they really suck at it, then it doesn't help you much.

I'm not saying that I'd be happy to work with someone who hates what they do.

What I am saying is that choosing a segment that you enjoy is important, but it won't be enough for your clients. You must make sure that segment is chock full of Magic.

To finish off the subject of your Magic, I'd like to offer you the following thought, in the hope that it might inspire you to shake off the shackles of erroneous motivation.

There is a lot written and spoken right now about "the power of why."

It's like one of those flavor-of-the-month things.

Mostly, it's all very true and very impactful. However, there is one erroneous misinterpretation which assigns furrowed brows to the foreheads of too many entrepreneurs.

The error is in failing to directly link their reason why they do what they do with their daily value delivery (a.k.a. "Magic").

For too many years, I worked with clients with the "why" of wanting to make enough money so that I could stop working with clients.

In your heart of hearts, without emailing me your confession, does this sound familiar?

For most entrepreneurs, it's all too familiar.

I know that most people write about how they love what they do and how they turn cartwheels between the car park and their office because they are overjoyed to serve humanity with the abundance of gifts that a gracious God has bestowed upon them.

But I'm betting dollars to donuts that most of them, in their quiet moments, would acknowledge that, if the business is not as wildly successful as they would like, they will be hoping and praying that they win lotto so that they can retire and do what they "really want to do."

And this is what I mean by the erroneous misinterpretation of the power of why.

The purest and strongest motivation, and therefore the most powerful why, that you can ever tap into, is to flip the switch in your brain that has you believing you should be someplace else (in retirement) and realize instead that you are exactly where you are meant to be, doing exactly what you're meant to be doing, and wake-up and go to your office every morning grateful and appreciative of the opportunities that you have.

Naturally, I invite you to be in love with the idea that you will get to enjoy the fruits of the work you do with your clients, but let me share with you a short story to illustrate the above point.

Around 15 years ago, I decided to compete in an Ironman triathlon.

That consists of a 3.8 km swim, or 180 km bike ride which is all a warmup for a full 42.2 km marathon.

It's not a goal which should be set lightly, because it's one tough day.

I got up five mornings a week, trained my butt off. I've always had a natural love of running, but the swimming and cycling training was always an effort.

One Sunday morning, I was up before the rest of the family and out the door on a cool clear autumn morning to spend six hours grinding up and down hills on my bike.

When I was about halfway through my training session, a motorcyclist zinged by me and I couldn't help but thinking "what the heck am I doing torturing myself with this training when I could be doing something that I absolutely love, which is being on a motorbike just like that one?"

I completed the triathlon and finished within the top third of the field, an achievement that I was happy with.

And I'm glad I've done it, but I wasn't doing going to do a second time.

I decided that in life there were inputs and outcomes.

The outcome that I was seeking was to complete an Ironman triathlon in a time that I could look back on and feel satisfied about.

The inputs consisted of a bucket load of swimming, cycling and running training.

With the exception of the running, I didn't want to do the inputs. But I had to do them because a lot of the outcome required that.

I decided that, for my next big goal, I was going to choose one where I enjoyed the inputs as much as the outcome.

So, I set a goal to race in the Australian Superbike Championships, having not put my bum on a motorbike for some 30 years prior.

But as mentioned above, I just love motorbikes and every Sunday when I woke up at 4 a.m. to get to the track on time for a day's practice, I had a smile on my dial, unlike the times that I woke up at 4 a.m. on a Sunday morning to grind out a 100 km cycle ride.

The moral of my story is for you to pick a Magic that allows you to genuinely enjoy the inputs (delivering value to your clients) as much as it affords you the ability to enjoy the fruits of your success, be that retirement or new house or taking your loved ones on a fabulous holiday.

Life is too short to give your head or your heart to a cause that you were not born to engage in. And passion around the inputs is your clue that you were born to do a certain thing.

So... pick one!

The Audiences

STRATEGIC QUESTION #2: WHO IS YOUR IDEAL CLIENT?

So NOW THAT you've identified your Magic, it's time to figure out how we're going to get a whole bunch of your ideal clients excited about benefiting from that Magic.

That's called marketing!

Every effective marketing system consists of many moving parts, but there are two main ones: Assets and Audiences.

To bring this concept to life, here's a simple example.

I have a relatively large email subscriber list and when I run free online training, such as a webinar on lead generation, I invite people on that list to attend.

In this example, the Audience comes from my list of email subscribers and the Asset is the PowerPoint presentation that I put together to present at the training webinar.

Take away either of those two parts, the list of invitees and the PowerPoint I use during the webinar, and nothing happens!

I am (almost painfully) aware that this is a very simple concept and will not come as news to you.

It will, however, help you in your high-level thinking about exactly where you are going to get your Audiences from, and which Assets you need to develop to be able to attract, engage, and convert people from prospect to client.

Of the two parts to this lead generation equation, getting the right Audience is a far tougher nut to crack than the Assets.

To illustrate this point, imagine that Sam is the world's best public speaker on the subject of business development.

He's funny, engaging, insightful, motivational and whatever other adjective you want to add that would make him, in your opinion, the world's best speaker. He also uses the stage to generate new client inquiries.

Then consider Pam, our other imaginary colleague.

She's not a great speaker. She mumbles about, cracks some jokes which go flat, and then proceeds to subject her Audience to "death by PowerPoint" with endless slides of bullet points.

But even though she is boring, it's clear that she knows her stuff, which happens to be the same stuff that Sam knows about: business development.

Now let's put Sam in front of a 100-strong Audience that is flat out broke and who are far more interested in when the free drinks are going to start than they are in the business development presentation.

And at the same time, we'll put Pam in front of a 100-strong Audience of folks who are actively seeking an expert on business development and who have the money to pay Pam her outrageously high fees. And we also imagine that for every member of the Audience now is the perfect time to start.

In those two scenarios, guess who is going to walk away with a bunch of new client inquiries?

Obviously, it's Pam.

The point of that little story is to underline and highlight and bold type the fact that without a quality Audience it doesn't matter how good an Asset you have.

Someone once said that the Audience is everything.

I wouldn't say that, but it comes pretty darned close to that.

Think about some of the traditionally recommended mediums that you could use to market your services.

A webinar?

No good without an Audience.

In fact, no good without the right Audience.

A book?

Ditto.

A survey?

Same deal.

I had a new client who wanted to put into place some lead generation systems and he told me that he spent $150,000 the previous year on a marketing consultant for the same purpose.

After 12 months work, the only significant thing that was left to show for the $150,000 was a new website which admittedly looked pretty good. I mean it was a work of art and even had some very cool graphics and super-seductive words on it.

Unfortunately, it was also like a million-dollar billboard in the middle of the Sahara.

What I am saying here is that having an Asset such as a genius-inspired website is of zero use whatsoever unless you can get the right people to visit.

(BTW: it's completely useless having visitors to your website unless you capture their contact details).

I could go on at this point, but I don't think you'll need me to.

The fact is that without an Audience, the right Audience, you will not generate new leads.

The best bait in the world is not going to pull any fish out of an empty pond.

We'll get to which lead generation Assets you need to develop very soon.

But for now, let's think about your Audiences and where you're going to get the right ones.

There is quite a lot of unnecessary training and instruction that's offered to help you form a demographic and psychographic profile of your ideal client.

But frankly, it shouldn't take you more than about three minutes.

Some of these courses ask you to write down the sort of watch they wear, the car they drive, or the style of the coffee they order. You don't need to know any of that.

You do need to know what their problem is and/or the challenges they face, what the symptoms of those problems/challenges are, what they have probably tried, and why it didn't work, but that's sufficient.

After that, all you need to know is that an ideal client has three characteristics:

1. They are aware of their need for your type of service.

2. They have the money to pay your fees.

3. The timing for them to invest with you is perfect.

Remove any one of those three criteria and they cease to be an "ideal" client.

Today I spoke to a client in South Africa. Jonnathan developed a seriously kick-ass algorithm that can locate hard to find skills/people together with their contact details and a social media en-riched report on each person.

Jonnathan software searches through some 3.8 billion people and compiles a list of the top 100 matches, based on customized search criterion, in around 30 seconds.

This is a pretty sexy product for professional recruiters or in-house recruitment executives.

Jonnathan had a business mentor at the meeting (which is invariably a double-edged sword) who raised multiple concerns about price shoppers, tire-kickers, multiple-stakeholder decision-makers and a whole lot more.

The mentor was concerned about how we should handle these difficult people.

I explained that we weren't going to even bother trying to handle such people.

I said that what we are going to do is to pick the "low-lying fruit," which is normally around 3 percent of the Audiences/market. The 3 percent possess the above three characteristics and they make decisions fast and they make decisions without reference to other stakeholders. And they are not difficult at all.

And until we pick all the low-lying fruit, we don't need to build a ladder.

That little story is offered in the hope of reinforcing a major marketing principle, which is that we don't have to be all things to all people.

In fact, we only want to be one thing (Magic) to the 3 percent of your potential market who possess the above three characteristics and are ready to rock 'n' roll with you.

I'll address the other 97 percent when we get to The Titanium Triangle and the SEW Segmentation formula later in this book.

But for now, you should know that the we can split that 97 percent into 12 percent and 85 percent segments.

The 12 percent are very similar to the 3 percent mentioned above in that they possess the same three characteristics, but they are not fast decision-makers like the 3 percent.

The 85 percent have no serious intention of buying, because they lack one or more of the above three characteristics.

That's not to say we want to ignore any of the previously mentioned three categories.

In fact, we want to get as many of them into your email database and connected with you on social media as we possibly can. And we want to BBB them too. (keep your Brand in their Brain until ready to Buy).

To do anything else would be wasting an opportunity.

But you should always build your initial lead generation system for the 3 percent who are ready to buy and simultaneously have some form of social media in place to BBB the 97 percent until they are ready to buy.

More on the latter, later.

Putting aside the above percentages for a moment, there are three main markets that my clients serve.

There is the corporate market (mostly executives), there is the consumer market (people living at home), and there is the small business/solopreneur market.

I'll dive into this in more detail when you look at which Assets you need to develop because the latter can vary depending on which market you serve.

For now, I simply need to let you know that, depending on which market you are serving (corporate, consumer or small business), you'll find your Audiences in different places.

By way of example, here is a sample list of just 8 places where you may be able to find a relevant Audience:

1. Your email list

2. Social Media followers (as distinct from LinkedIn connections)

3. Other Peoples' Networks

4. Amazon

5. Facebook

6. Messenger

7. LinkedIn

8. Conferences

9. Search Engine Optimization

10. AdWords

Let's go through some of these and have a look at their relative potential.

1. YOUR EMAIL LIST

Chances are you don't have one. Very few people do.

I'm not talking about people in your Outlook or iCal software, I am talking about people who have subscribed to your email list and have given you permission to contact them with added-value opportunities and/or special offers.

Most of my new clients choose to use platforms such as MailChimp to start with because it's completely free and does a pretty good job in terms of providing a database for people who have opted in on your website (in exchange for a free report or similar) and then allow you the facility to bulk email them with invitations to online or off-line events.

And that's a reason why Outlook and iCal are not adequate as databases for email campaigns. You can't send hundreds of emails out at once from Outlook or iCal and, even if you could, neither of them complies with anti-spam regulations which allow people to quickly and easily find the unsubscribe link.

Currently I have around 13,000 people on my subscriber list. That's not big by some standards, but I'd rather have 100 highly engaged subscribers than 100,000 disengaged subscribers. Literally.

So please don't be impressed with the size of anyone's list; it's the quality that counts.

Having said that, the bigger your list of engaged subscribers, the better.

Most people don't start a list because they stall themselves with the idea that they don't have enough people to start a list.

Here's my advice: sign up for MailChimp or MailerLite or whatever platform reviews well and that you can kick off with a free trial.

Then block out four hours in your scheduler to go through your email contacts and whatever files you might have off-line, and make a list of everyone you've done business with in the past, everyone who has met with you to discuss business, any relevant suppliers, current clients, relevant industry contacts, and so on.

In short, we're looking for people with whom you have an established business relationship (whether they were clients or not), which gives you the legal and ethical permission you need to add them to your online email database.

Put all those contacts, including first name and email address as a minimum, into a spreadsheet and then you can quickly and easily import that list into the email platform/database that you've signed up for.

Goethe wrote that "Boldness has genius, power and magic in it" and urged that whatever we sought to undertake, we should "begin it!".

I'm sure that when Goethe wrote those words in 1808 he wasn't thinking about email platforms, but nevertheless I am pretty sure he'd apply the same "just get started" sentiment to that subject.

2. SOCIAL MEDIA FOLLOWERS (AS DISTINCT FROM LINKEDIN CONNECTIONS)

Social Media is a very weak medium through which to generate new client inquiries.

I've said it before but is worth repeating that Social Media is regarded as being a highly valuable method for keeping your Brand in the marketplace's Brain (the 97 percent discussed above) until ready to buy.

Outside of that, the major Social Media platforms such as Facebook, YouTube, Twitter, Instagram, and Pinterest don't represent the fastest or most effective medium through which to generate fresh leads.

I would gladly swap 100,000 Facebook (or LinkedIn) connections for 1,000 highly engaged subscribers.

3. OTHER PEOPLES NETWORKS (OPN)

This is where the gold is.

And the gold is largely free.

And you need do very little digging to find it.

You just need to know where to dig.

I've personally generated millions of dollars in revenue through OPN and I would imagine that, collectively, those clients who I have trained on OPN would have generated tens, if not hundreds of millions.

But OPN is like a combination safe.

Just like a safe, the treasure lies inside and it's really not hard to access, if you have the right combination.

But just like the combination code for opening a safe, one wrong turn will keep you shut out from the treasure.

So, would you like the code?

I bet you would!

I'm going to give you a series of steps that you can combine to crack open the OPN safe.

Here goes.

STEP ONE: Figure out who else has a database full of your potential ideal clients. You're looking for an individual, not an organization or an association. The latter represents safes like Fort Knox — lots of people want to get in, but is just too hard to crack.

Instead, look for people who feature themselves on their websites with head and shoulder photos, who are active in social media and who have an up-to-date and highly professional LinkedIn profile.

And look for people who are marketing a complementary service into the same marketplace as yours.

For example, my client Dawn in Perth, Australia, has an ideal client profile of senior execs who understand that their teams have massive productivity upside if only they were more engaged.

Dawn's potential OPN partners would include anyone else offering professional training and programs into the same market. They could be time management experts, recruitment consultants, and performance appraisal experts and so on.

They would not include anyone offering physical products into the same market. That never works because there is a disconnect in the mind of the market between someone offering a physical product such as computers or desks or car leases, versus a specialist consultant or trainer who offers services and/or advice.

STEP TWO: Invoke the law of psychological reciprocity by doing something totally cool for the potential OPN partners you identified in Step One.

The phenomenon of psychological reciprocity simply means that as human beings we like to keep the "giving score" even.

In other words, somebody does something valuable for you then you'll feel unconsciously obliged to do something valuable for them in return, should the opportunity present itself, and should all other things be equal: e.g., ethical and legal considerations.

You've got to be genuine about this, but if you respect the other person's work and feel that your network (remember that email list you just started?) would value their insights, then you can do things like re-post their blogs (and make sure they know about it), or retweet their tweets, or post a positive review for their book and so on.

Do not, under any circumstances, do anything to damage your reputation as an honest, straightforward professional, such as endorsing their skills on LinkedIn, when in fact you've never even met the other person, let alone worked with them.

In the interests of full disclosure, I'm not going to declare my lack of full disclosure (I invite you to read that again) — I have a "secret sauce recipe" for activating psychological reciprocity in the minds of potential foes, but I'm not prepared to lay it all out in this book.

Sorry!

There are two things that prevent me from revealing my secret sauce in this book.

Thing number one is that often, unless we pay for something, we don't value it. If I were to share the recipe with you here and now, there's a very high probability that you would skip ahead to some other shiny thing. But if you paid for the recipe... well, that's a different story.

Thing number two is that this particular secret sauce is so valuable that I'd be an idiot to give it away.

But I like to think that I've given you the principle for opening the OPN safe, if not the exact prescription.

What I have suggested above <u>will</u> get you started.

In the meantime, I will give you a litmus test that you want to use in real life OPN situations before you use Step Three in the marketplace.

Here's the test: if you were to call this potential OPN host on their mobile phone and they saw that it was you calling and assuming that they weren't busy, would they pick up and happily greet you?

If the answer to that question is no, either because they have no idea who you are or because they don't like the idea of talking to you, then you're not ready for Step Three, so you go back to building psychological reciprocity.

Proceeding to Step Three prior to passing the above litmus test is more than likely to turn your OPN host target completely off the idea of any form of communication or engagement with you.

It's the equivalent of going up to a relative stranger and asking them to marry you. Not too many people can pull that off apart from maybe George Clooney and Heidi Klum.

STEP THREE: Make your potential OPN host an offer that is too good to refuse.

You can offer to promote their book, you can offer to host them at a webinar, you can offer to promote the landing page that they want to drive some traffic to.

Were after a no-brainer type offer.

And there must be no strings attached do your offer. Even though you have the idea that you'd love to get your Message into their database, you mentally put that aside for the time being.

Instead, with Step Three, you move from Step Two by ramping up psychological reciprocity and do something even cooler for them, but you mentally put scissors through the strings that connect what you're doing for them with what you want them to do for you in Step Four.

STEP FOUR: Suggest some cross marketing.

The easiest way to get a potential OPN host to market something of yours to their list, is by what I call the Prius Factor.

When Toyota launched the hybrid vehicle they call a Prius, they stuck their hybrid engine into what many regarded as an ugly body. Whether it was ugly or not is open to opinion, but no one could argue that the car's shape was certainly distinctive.

When Honda launched their hybrid vehicle, they simply called it a Honda Accord Hybrid. Honda's car looked identical to the millions of other Honda Accords on the road. The only difference was a small red badge that read "Hybrid" next to the pre-existing Accord badge on the rear of the car.

Toyota outsold Honda by more than 10 to 1.

When the marketing researchers finished their work, they discovered that the reason for Toyota's runaway success was that buyers of hybrid vehicles wanted one thing more than being environmentally friendly.

They wanted to be *seen* to be environmentally friendly.

And that wasn't going to happen by using a small red badge stuck on the back of a car that look the same as millions of others.

Now listen up, and listen up good…

Because what I'm about to tell you is pure gold.

Once you get to Step Four, you invoke the ghost of that first Prius model and come up with an offer for your potential OPN host that makes them look freaking awesome in front of their Audience/email list.

Granted, this may take a little work on your behalf.

But I cracked the code on this one and I can tell you that one of the easiest ways to have potential OPN hosts offer their lists, after you've built psychological reciprocity, is something like **www. fivehourchallenge.com.**

The beauty about that offer is firstly that my potential OPN host, who by this stage thinks that I'm one of the good guys, can validate the quality of my work quickly and easily by me sending them a link to the five short videos that their list is going to be invited to opt-in for.

Think about this: you must minimize the risk of your offer and maximize the reward in the mind of your potential OPN host.

In the example given above, they checked out the quality and they know that what I'm offering is valuable, and that minimizes the risk of any negative feedback from their list.

In terms of maximizing reward, they are very likely to have their subscribers thank them for introducing them to this opportunity.

By contrast, if I suggest to a potential OPN host that they invite their list to attend an event (off-line or online) that I'll speak at, the risk is much higher in their mind.

You'll strike resistance from every single potential OPN host unless you:

- Identify potential hosts who offer complimentary services versus competitive services.

- Build psychological reciprocity to the point where they would cheerfully answer their mobile phone when they saw it was you calling.

- Create an offer that makes them look good in front of their Audience and eliminates any risk factor.

OPN deserves your 100 percent commitment and persistence.

The payoff for you cracking the OPN safe is significant and has the potential to create what is an inexhaustible supply of new leads, because you can use the same combination to get into safe after safe after safe.

You need to first build an OPN process that works.

You then need to make it as efficient as possible.

You then need to make it even more effective.

You then document that process.

You then outsource as many parts of it as humanly possible.

You then sit back and wake up to more subscribers and more new client inquiries.

And remember that with OPN you pay for zero advertising on Facebook or anywhere else, you've grown your subscriber list significantly with people who are interested in what you've got, and you can do all this in a minimum of time with zero stress, seamlessly and smoothly, because you've now got a proven system that you can "rinse and repeat" happily ever after.

And that, my friend, is a beautiful thing.

4. AMAZON

As you probably know, Amazon is the world's largest retailer.

Yes, it's an online retailer but in many respects, it works the same as a physical retail store.

Imagine one extraordinarily large retail store that was so big it sold 74 percent of the world's transactions.

(In fact, Amazon has 74 percent market share for e-commerce, so not quite the same thing, but still it's close enough to reinforce the point that I'm about to make.)

And imagine that it was possible to make your product magically visible in that store to only those people who fit your ideal client profile.

And imagine that, instead of you having to handle the logistics of getting your product into that retail store, and managing the invoicing and collection of sales revenue, and handling stock and inventory in a warehouse, the store handled all of that for you.

And imagine that not only did that store take all those hassles out of your hands, but they actually manufactured your product for you without charging you a cent.

And imagine that they paid you proceeds from each sale of your product at a multiple of four times more than the other retail stores would pay you.

Are you getting excited yet?

You should be!

Every year, Amazon sells $5.25 billion worth of books.

The paperback version of this book is printed by Amazon (actually, their subsidiary "Createspace") on demand and shipped out to buyers without me lifting a finger.

In the bad old days, I would have had 10,000 copies printed in Hong Kong and shipped to my garage here in Australia, where that stockpile would slowly dwindle to the point where we might even be able to get a car back in.

And I would be responsible for mailing out every copy and I would be responsible for facing my wife periodically to explain why her car was sitting out in the weather.

No thanks!

And if you purchased the Kindle copy of this book, then you're helping to make up the 65 percent of market share that Amazon has in e-books.

My very first book was picked up by a North American publisher who paid me less than two dollars on a $30 sale. Amazon pays me eight dollars when they sell a $30 book for me, and they pay on time every single month as regular as a Swiss clock.

Hopefully by now, I've got you excited about how easy it is to have your book sold on Amazon.

But why would you want to write a book, I hear you ask.

There's a whole bunch of reasons, including the fact that once you are a published author (it really doesn't matter a hoot whether you're self-published or published by the publisher), you gain more credibility as being a specialist expert in the area of your Magic.

Especially if you become a bestseller, which is certainly in the cards if you do an excellent job of writing the book.

This book is not really a book. It's more like the Trojan horse.

You bought the book thinking that you were buying a book.

When in fact, as mentioned in the Preface, what you're really investing in is my opportunity to convince you that paying a multiple of whatever you paid for this book is a really clever idea.

(Rest assured, whether or not we ever end up working together, you will have still received more than full value for your investment in this book.)

Books are an extraordinarily effective way to establish your brand in the brain of your marketplace, and books give you the time that you need with each prospect to convince them that you are their number-one best option for solving their problem or realizing the potential of their challenge.

My book sells every month without me lifting a finger.

Inquiries come in regularly from people who turn out to be very high-quality clients.

It's all very scalable and the financial costs of getting the book onto Amazon would be no greater than $500 for typesetting and having a graphic artist create a cover (add another $500 to that if you want to have the book proofread).

Getting your book on Amazon will give you one of the highest return on investment of any of your marketing efforts.

Provided you write the book in an engaging manner, and you can achieve that by following my proprietary Leadsology® Persuasion Sequence coming up in Part Four.

5. FACEBOOK

When you think about it, there is such an abundance of Audiences that it could easily feel like you're surrounded by them.

The question is therefore not "where do I find my Audience?" but rather "which Audience is the best one to focus on and how do I get the Message about my Magic into that Audience?"

Having said that, Facebook may not be the right Audience for you.

However, with a staggering 2.01 billion monthly active users, 1.57 billion daily mobile users, 1.32 billion daily desktop users and an estimated 50 percent of online seniors together with 40 million small businesses that have a Facebook page and over 100 million hours of video watched every day… Facebook is an opportunity that is definitely worthy of your consideration.

And it would be wrong to think that Facebook will only generate leads for you if you're in the consumer market.

I have clients who have generated seriously high-quality corporate clients using Facebook advertisements.

You and I both know that people don't go to Facebook with the intention of buying something. Not yet, at least, although I'd suggest you "watch this space" because Zuckerberg is definitely moving the platform in that direction.

Facebook captures the market that I referred to as the Wanderers. These are the people who go to Facebook to catch up on the news from friends and family and then see a shiny thing which could be in the form of your advertisement or your post.

Because if you do a great job with the image that catches their eye, and a great job on the headline that features a benefit of interest to them, they may click on the link and find themselves on your landing page.

To give you an idea, here's an example of such a landing page: **www.fivehourchallenge.com**

Once on your landing page, they can opt-in to your list and off you go from there keeping the Brand in the Brain until they are ready to Buy.

As mentioned previously, I've recently abandoned Facebook advertising because it's become quite expensive. That may or may not prove to be the case for you.

If you're prepared to do a lot of hard work on a continuing basis, then you may get an acceptable return on your advertising investment with Facebook (or indeed Instagram or LinkedIn or Pinterest).

And even if Facebook wasn't the medium through which you enjoyed the best return on investment, you may still choose to advertise on it because it still gives you a significant return.

In addition to Facebook advertising, there are also Facebook groups.

You should definitely check out and join the Leadsology® Facebook group at **www.Facebook.com/groups/leadsology/** so you can gain an insight into how Facebook groups can be used to cultivate prospects as well as generate new client inquiries and indeed, make sales.

I'm not a huge fan of using a personal Facebook page as a medium for marketing your business. I know that some Facebook experts recommend that people like me post photos of myself cliff diving in Acapulco, sitting on the hood of my Aston Martin in the driveway in front of my beach-side mansion, and smiling happily amidst a flock of beautiful women hanging off both arms.

The idea is that I should be creating a visual message so that prospective clients will think "I want what he's got and if I pay him money then I too will be able to cliff dive in Acapulco, pose on the hood of an expensive car and have highly desirable potential mating partners salivating at the prospect of copulating with me."

Something like that.

And I can't be bothered.

Firstly, because it would be totally disingenuous. Yes, I live in one of the most fabulous locations in the world on the sand next to a beach, but no, I don't have any desire to own an expensive and big brand car, and the only woman I want hanging off my arm is my wife, who is unapologetically unavailable... I hope.

6. MESSENGER BOTS

These days, email marketers are doing well if they send out an email blast to their subscribers and have 20 percent of recipients open the email.

It would be an email marketer's idea of heaven if those rates could climb to 50 percent.

Right now, Facebook Messenger is delivering more than 97 percent open rates.

That's seriously impressive.

Especially when you consider that it's highly likely that the majority of your prospects are included in the 900 million people using Messenger every month, and at the time of this writing, the platform is still only six years old.

So, what's a bot?

A bot is a term used to describe pretty much any software that automates a digital task.

Chatbots, which you or I can now build on Facebook Messenger, automate conversations, or at the very least, the start of a conversation.

What's especially clever about bots is that they can be fully customized and used by clients to order a bunch of flowers and have them delivered to a specific address, or to get livestock quotes from the *Wall Street Journal* or receive advice on a medical issue.

For us marketers, bots can be used to engage targeted prospects with free offers that lead them to a landing page which in turn can capture their email details, or have them register for an off-line event, or simply attend a live stream training with an offer at the end to meet and discuss their specific needs.

Marketing with bots is still a relatively new phenomenon, but as a potential Audience it's not one that any of us should ignore.

Two more things to consider about bots:

Because this medium is in its infancy, there is going to be an awful lot of hype around it and a lot of claims made by people wanting to sell you their bot-making services.

Be careful before you part with your hard-earned money!

Ask for either a guarantee of satisfaction, or a guarantee of results. If anyone promises to give you the combination to the bot-safe without a guarantee, be wary — be very wary.

I'm not a great believer in outsourcing your marketing. This strategy normally ends in tears. Mostly, you are best to develop your own lead-generation systems, as outlined in this book, get them working really well, and then outsource the parts of them that you can.

Similarly, if you want to get into the world of bots, what I recommend is that you find someone who can work with you, step-by-step, and show you how to build your own custom bot.

The downside of trying to outsource an entire lead generation system from the get go, is that you are very much flying in the dark as to whether the contractor that you've selected is very good at what they do, or simply very good at marketing what they allege they do. Unfortunately, the latter is all too often the case.

7. LinkedIn

Wow, where to begin?

Maybe with the numbers, which looks something like this:

467 million — Number of members

106 million — Number of monthly active users

1.5 Million — The total number of Groups

40 percent — Members who use LinkedIn daily

3 million — Number of LinkedIn users sharing content weekly

79 percent — Business-to-business marketers who view LinkedIn as an effective source for generating leads

92 percent — Business-to-business marketers who leverage LinkedIn over all other social platforms

930 — LinkedIn connections for the average CEO

71 percent — Professionals who feel that LinkedIn is a credible source for professional content

Technically, LinkedIn is more of a business network than a social network. Unlike Facebook, people actually log in to LinkedIn to connect with other professionals for recruitment, educational, or prospecting reasons.

No conversation about Audiences would be complete without addressing this extraordinarily massive pool of potential.

LinkedIn was launched in 2002 and traded its first shares in 2011, at which point it had certainly come of age. It was acquired just a smidgen over five years later by Microsoft for $26.2 billion; such was their view of the potential synergy between the two companies.

Without doubt, the greatest Asset that LinkedIn has is its members. I don't imagine for a moment that the revenue flow from LinkedIn advertising, or indeed any other revenue flowing into LinkedIn, were significant factors in Microsoft's calculation as to what they were prepared to pay for LinkedIn.

As I demonstrated earlier, if you've got the wrong Audience, you've got a snowball's chance in hell of getting any clients from it.

But if you've got the right Audience, then you have the potential for building Assets to tap into the demand for your services that will inevitably exist in an Audience as large as LinkedIn.

I'm embarrassed to say that it took me years to figure out the combination to the LinkedIn safe.

I bought courses, completed training programs, attended workshops, and read books.

I mean, who hasn't?

And I'll bet you dollars to donuts (once again) that you've dabbled with the thought of how to get into that particular safe.

My conclusion was that the people making the most money out of LinkedIn were the people selling the courses, programs and books on how to make money out of LinkedIn.

If I can use a mining analogy, it's like the old days of gold rushes where a vast majority of prospectors went home broken and broke, but the suppliers of rudimentary equipment such as picks, shovels, tents and hand-held sluicing equipment made most of the money.

We all know that there is gold inside the LinkedIn safe, but how the heck do you get some of that wealth into your own bank account?

I am pleased to say that after nine very focused months of trialing and failing, I figured out the combination and I'll reveal that to you in Part Three of this book.

In the meantime, let me assure you with a 100 percent cast iron guarantee, that sending a message to thousands of connections on LinkedIn, inviting them to download your thingy, whatever that may be, or to attend your event or to buy your downloadable PDF, and so on, isn't going to work.

A colleague of mine claims to have more than 60,000 1st level connections on LinkedIn. He explains that he grew his network before LinkedIn placed a cap on the number of connections at 30,000.

He offered to host a webinar where I would present about lead generation and he told me that he would message all his LinkedIn contacts to fill the webinar.

We had eight people show up.

That gives you a significantly important insight into what NOT to expect from LinkedIn.

While we're on the subject of LinkedIn, earlier I discussed the option of appointment-setters who traditionally use LinkedIn for prospecting purposes to set up meetings for you with potential clients.

The problem with outsourcing to appointment-setters (or to anyone else for that matter) is that the thing upon which your future security relies (lead generation) is now completely outside of your control and that's a scary thought.

If you're going to be in control of your financial future, then you need to be in control of your lead generation.

So instead of outsourcing LinkedIn marketing, you're far better off to work with someone and learn how to implement each lead-generation system so that you retain ultimate control over those systems and, therefore, ultimate control of your financial destiny.

Cliched but true: better to be taught how to fish than to be given a fish.

More on LinkedIn soon.

8. CONFERENCES

In the previous part of this book I covered the reasons why I'm not a big fan of running my own marketing events, but speaking at someone else's conference or event can be very worthwhile.

I launched one very successful business in 1995 using nothing more than bulk faxing (very cost-effective) and bulk direct postal mail (expensive but worthwhile at the time).

As mentioned previously, we typically sent out thousands of invitations to attend a free seminar, paid for the cost of buying the list of names, the cost of the mail out, the cost of hiring a conference room, the cost of the audio/visual gear, the cost of refreshments for our guests, and the cost of having someone to register them and so on.

The reason I took the time and trouble and expense to run these meetings was simple: they worked.

If we got 100 people registered to an event, 67 would turn up, 26 would use a feedback form to indicate that they wanted to meet and talk about whether our services were a fit for their needs, 20 would show up to those meetings and eight would sign up for our $3,000 a year service, on the spot.

But that was over 20 years ago.

A small thing called the Internet has grown just a tad since then, and it makes what was then a necessity of running my own marketing events, now an optional extra.

But while I have mostly abandoned the cost, complexity and effort of running my own marketing events, I still seek selected opportunities to speak on the stage at conferences and other events where the Audience is a match with my ideal client profile.

Think about it: I have none of the expense or effort of getting the Audience into that room, but I have exactly the same opportunity to strut my stuff, impress the socks off the 3 percent of the room that are ready to buy from me, and most of the time, get paid pretty well for that opportunity.

There is a strong trend these days to set up conferences and then charge the speakers to present to the Audience.

I dislike that idea because the conference organizers tend to lose sight of the need to seek out quality presenters. They get blinded by potentially lower-quality presenters who can't get themselves invited to speak at quality conferences and instead simply wave a big check in the face of the organizer.

Also, it just feels wrong.

The message and the way I deliver it needs to be important enough and engaging enough and valuable enough for organizers and Audiences for what it is, as opposed to being average enough that I need to pay for that opportunity.

Having said that, what this trend underscores is the value that many marketers place on the opportunity to speak at conferences.

But there's a catch.

Advertising agencies will often talk about two types of marketing strategies: push and pull.

Push marketing is where a business attempts to proactively and directly market a product to customers. For example, a manufacturer of a perfume line may provide sales incentives to retail staff, engage in advertising campaigns such as a two for one sale, put up elaborate point-of-sale displays and so on.

Pull marketing takes the opposite approach. The idea is that we get the marketplace to do a good chunk of the marketing for us in the form of word-of-mouth referrals, formal referral programs, customer loyalty cards, air points, and ongoing special offers to existing clients. An example of this is DropBox, the cloud-based storage solution that offered users and their referrals free bonus storage space, and in doing so created pull-through of new customers through their existing ones.

The reason I mention these two different marketing strategies is it takes massively less effort to secure conference speaking gigs once you've built a reputation for being a great speaker and thereby get invited to speak, as opposed to laboriously approaching conference organizers and spruiking yourself as God's answer to their problem of finding the good speakers.

On that note, allow me to introduce you to the late great Debbie Tawes who owned Celebrity Speakers, a booking agency where conference organizers would go to find good speakers.

Around 22 years ago, I attended a professional speakers' association meeting where Debbie was the speaker. She bluntly and directly told the Audience of wannabe- speakers (which included me) not to call her and ask to get booked. She said that she would let us know that was not the way the speaking industry worked.

How it works, she said, was that when her phone was ringing off the hook with people asking her if she could book you, then, and only then, would she want to speak with you.

It was a classic "don't call me, I'll call you."

So, you have two options in regard to speaking at other people's meetings: pull marketing where you approach say 10 conference organizers every week and ask them if they want to book you. Fifty percent of them will respond and say that they would love to book you and that all you need to do is pay them $5,000 and you're in. Twenty-five percent will ignore you and 25 percent will tell you to come back next year.

Good luck with that plan!

It's hard yards and requires an extraordinary amount of persistence and volume to yield even one gig.

Personally, I'd rather take the shortcut which, ironically, takes more time.

In other words, I'd recommend that you use my proprietary Lead-sology® Persuasion Sequence to create a great talk, get some gigs at local, small, business networking meetings, knock their socks off, generate some leads, convert them into clients, write a best-selling book, get interviewed by a hundred podcasters and then wait for the conference organizers to contact you.

Which they will.

Of course, when I say this is a shortcut, it's not a shortcut that's going to get you speaking gigs faster; it is a shortcut in that it'll get you better-quality speaking gigs that are paid (important word) and gigs that position you as a genuinely sought-after, in-demand expert, faster than spamming or cold-calling conference organizers.

In Bruce Springsteen's autobiography, he writes about the long period of time before he was famous, when he was broke and desperate to get any gig that he could.

He was offered a gig in New York, but he didn't have a car, so he borrowed one and drove to New York. When he hit the turnpike/tollgate just out of New York, he ran into trouble. There was a large sign that he said was all too familiar with, which read "No Pennies."

All Springsteen had was pennies. Reluctantly, the woman at the turnpike said she would accept them and after he dumped them into her hands, she then counted them out laboriously, one at a time.

She then announced that he was one cent short and she wasn't gonna let him through until she had the full dollar.

Springsteen got out of his car and got on his hands and knees and searched under the seats seeking that elusive last penny.

All the while cars were backing up behind them, with people sticking their heads out the windows and yelling out, tooting their horns and generally getting all steamed up.

Finally, Springsteen found the last cent, gave it to the woman and she let them through.

To this day, Springsteen repeats his mantra to up-and-coming performers: "you need the full dollar to get into New York," which I am going to use as an analogy for needing to be damn good at what you do before you can get entry to the "Glory Days" of getting booked for paid speaking gigs.

9. SEARCH ENGINE OPTIMIZATION (SEO)

The idea with SEO is that, when someone goes to a search engine like Google, and searches for your services, you'd ideally pop up as one of the top three or four in the list of websites that was compiled as a result of their search.

There are two categories of SEO which are on-site and off-site.

On-site SEO includes things like incorporating the words that people are searching for when looking for your service, into your website "URL" address.

Google also takes note of the age of your website, with older websites ranking better than newer ones. Also, the frequency that the phrases or words being searched for appear on your website will affect your rankings.

Off-site SEO includes everything outside your website which helps you rank well in search results.

For example, if a government website or an education website publishes a link to your website (referred to as a backlink), that's going to help with your search rankings. In short, the more backlinks you have from credible websites the better your website will rank in searches.

I could write a small encyclopedia on SEO, but I'm not going to because the purpose of this little section is simply to let you know whether you should bother with SEO.

There is a fair chance that if you are offering professional services, advice, or software, I'd recommend you not waste time and money on SEO, which is why it's on the list of 10 traditionally recommended marketing methods that you should probably avoid, at least initially.

However, if you decide that focusing on SEO as a source of new leads is a promising idea, then do yourself a favor and find an agency that is extremely good at it and work with them over a period of months or years to bring it to life.

By the way, having SEO work completed by an outside agency is one of the exceptions to my rule of not outsourcing your marketing. That's because, unlike say appointment-setters, once the SEO work has been completed, and you are ranking well for searches, then you are not dependent on the agency in the long term.

There is quite a lot involved to be effective at SEO, and the game is changing all the time as Google adjusts its search algorithms in its attempt to give people increasingly accurate results from their search request.

That said, I can tell you the basics of what you need to know about SEO in fairly short order.

If you have a local service, then you should definitely have some SEO work done.

For example, my wife is an acupuncturist.

She has long-term, die-hard clients who know just how effective her treatments are and who are prepared to literally travel for hours to see her.

However, the vast majority of her prospective new clients are not prepared to travel for more than 20 minutes to come and see her.

This is a classic case where SEO work is worthwhile.

I've had her website optimized for the phrase "Noosa acupuncture," so that when someone completes a Google search for that phrase in our local area (this therefore may not work where you live), then her website will pop up in the top two websites listed by Google.

In addition to grabbing the URL **www.Noosaacupuncture.com** (incorporating the most commonly searched for phrase by her potential clients), we did a little bit of other work, including gaining a handful of five-star Google reviews.

Contrast that scenario of a specialist in small geographical area with my client Paul in London who brokers acquisition deals between large international corporate clients and smaller technology companies.

It's very difficult for Paul to make SEO work for him, and also tough for him to be able to generate any credibility whether his website is found on the first page of the Google search or not.

Corporate execs looking to invest $1 billion or more in an acquisition aren't going to be swayed into doing business with Paul simply because he ranks well in a Google search.

So, if you're like my wife, and you have a local business offering a specialty, whether that's acupuncture or plumbing or accounting services, then SEO make sense.

For the vast majority of others, I'd recommend that you save your money, save your time, and save yourself a whole lot of frustration and forget about it.

And if you do connect with an SEO expert who promises to drive a flow of traffic to your website, then once again, make sure that they are taking the risk and not you.

In other words, check and see if they're offering some sort of guarantee, either a guarantee of results, or a guarantee of satisfaction.

Either way, you want the ball to be in your court as to whether their services are worth what you are paying money for, after you engage them.

And just a reminder that you would do well to consider such risk mitigation or risk reversal strategies for your own services, so that you remove yet another one of those speed bumps on the road that a prospective client journeys down as they explore the opportunity of working with you.

10. AdWords

Also known as Pay-Per-Click (PPC), Google ad words is a platform run by Google that allows you to advertise your website in search results when a user searches for a specific keyword.

When you use PPC successfully, the advertisement and link for your website will normally appear on the right-hand side of the search results page, and/or at the top above the list of organic searches (see SEO above).

The success of both SEO and AdWords critically depends on the correct selection of those keywords.

So, when should you use SEO versus AdWords?

If you have a business that services a very small geographic area like my wife with her acupuncture practice, then the chances are that, with a little bit of SEO work, your website will rank in the top three or four listings for organic search results ("organic" being non-paid versus the PPC//AdWords results), which is what you need to aim for.

If, however, you are like my client Sean, who is a foreclosure attorney in Philadelphia, and who covers a very large population area of some 6 million with literally hundreds of competitors, and the people searching for your type of service are very specific in what they're looking for (in this case preventing a bank or finance company from foreclosing on their home), then AdWords can open your business up to a tremendously profitable Audience.

The Message

STRATEGIC QUESTION #3: WHAT'S THE MESSAGE ABOUT YOUR MAGIC THAT YOU WANT YOUR AUDIENCE TO HEAR?

THERE'S A LOT written about developing your Unique Sales Proposition or USP as it's come to be known.

The idea is that you create a short statement which succinctly articulates, in a highly differentiated manner, the core value that you offer to your ideal clients.

The concept of USP was developed in the 1940s as a theory to explain why some advertising campaigns were more successful than others.

As far as I'm aware, it was first articulated by legendary television advertising guru, Rosser Reeves. With a name like that, he was always destined to end up in advertising!

Since time immemorial, marketers have known what Coco Chanel so eloquently stated which was that *"in order to be indispensable one must be different."*

Rosser Reeves was on the money with his idea, both metaphorically and literally.

But USP has suffered from the phenomenon we call "Chinese whispers" in that, over the last 80 years, the original formulation has been passed on so many times that it's almost unrecognizable when presented in more-recent books and workshops.

And so, despite the widespread teaching and training about the USP concept, 99 percent of businesses (and I do mean that number literally) are bereft of any marketing message that encapsulates the full power of the original USP concept.

In 1997, when I was marketing and running a three-year personal and business development program, I came up with the USP *"creating the life you deserve,"* which I modified shortly thereafter.

The reason I modified it was that I was having dinner with a lawyer in Sydney Australia and he asked me what I did for a living and so I thought it would be the perfect time to trot out my USP and so I told him "I help you create the life you deserve".

"Hell!" he exclaimed, "as a lawyer, that's the last thing I want!"

So, I changed it to *"creating the life you desire."*

But in my heart of hearts, I knew it wasn't enough.

It wasn't compelling, it wasn't magnetic, it didn't really stand out as being dramatically different from all the self-help gurus running around.

Since then I've had quite a few years to think more deeply about a formula for creating a USP that really packed a punch.

The first thing I that I decided is that we should remove the word "sales" from the term Unique Sales Proposition for no other reason than I don't particularly like it.

To me, even though I cut my commercial teeth in the world of selling life insurance, I very much prefer the idea that we can be smart enough to have the leads coming in to us, rather than us having to go out into the marketplace and convince otherwise unconvinced people that they need what we've got.

And so it was in 2009 that I came up with both the definition and a formula for creating more effective marketing messages.

It's probably important that at this point I put what little modesty I have remaining to one side, and let you know that my work on marketing messages has been internationally recognized as something of a breakthrough, both in the academic and commercial worlds.

Consequently, this is not something I cooked up yesterday or thought might look nice in the book to fill up a bitter white space.

For example, my client Derek, who markets into one of the toughest markets in the world, that of high-level vice presidents and CEOs of some of the world's biggest food and beverage corporations, experienced a transformation in his results once he followed my formula for creating an effective marketing message.

"Whereas before it was difficult in the extreme to get the attention of my ideal clients, I now have a pipeline full of inquiries which have come in from the vice presidents of some of the world's largest corporations."

And that's the power of an effective marketing message.

My experience is that the creation of an effective marketing message is a journey rather than a destination. As human beings we are wired to want completion and have a thing finished.

But with marketing messages, we have to change them whenever we gain deeper insight into the more specific needs that our ideal clients possess.

We also need to change them when competitors move in on our territory.

And we need to change them when marketplace needs or consumer preferences change.

Creating a marketing message is not a set-it-and-forget-it type of thing.

I wish it was, but truth be told, I've changed mine twice in the last 15 months alone.

WHERE TO USE YOUR MARKETING MESSAGE

To give the subject of marketing messages some context, it's important that you know where we're heading with this.

Every single effective marketing Asset has an effective marketing message embedded in it.

For example, you need look no further than the cover of this book, which promises to reveal a proven model for enjoying a weekly flow of new client inquiries.

Or go to one of my landing pages, such as **www.fivehourchallenge.com** and read the title.

Or read the title from one of my webinars: "How To Generate At Least 10 Fresh Referrals Every Month."

It's likely that just about every bestselling marketing book on Amazon has an effective marketing message embedded into the title.

So, what makes the marketing message effective versus ineffective?

To answer the question, we first must create a benchmark in the form of what we want to achieve with the marketing message.

And I humbly suggest, after more than a decade of playing with this thing, that there are two primary objectives which, when achieved, tell us that we have an effective marketing message.

OBJECTIVE NUMBER ONE IS TO GET THE ATTENTION OF OUR AUDIENCE

(Remember, when I use the term Audience, I'm referring to your ideal clients and not necessarily a literal bunch of people sitting on seats waiting to hear you speak).

OBJECTIVE NUMBER TWO IS TO MOTIVATE YOUR AUDIENCE TO TAKE ACTION

Not just any action of course, but the action that represents taking one step closer to booking a time to talk with you about your services.

I read a statement the other day that 79 percent of our buying decisions are made at the point when people read the title of a product or service featured on a website.

That is so far from the truth that it's funny.

The idea is based on the common misconception that people buy because they *feel* something.

Of course, emotions play a part in most buying decisions, but emotions form only 20 percent of the buying process in the marketplace in which most of my clients play.

That's because most of my clients are selling to either corporate buyers or small business owners/solopreneurs.

These are invariably mature, sophisticated, thinking, experienced, skeptical, time-poor and stressed people who have been burnt before.

And none of them are going to hand over $50,000 or so based on "feeling" something.

I often say to clients when we create an Asset, such as a book or a webinar or a pitch or presentation, that 20 percent of what we are doing is getting the Audience to feel something, especially initially.

And that the other 80 percent is explaining rationally and logically how your service works (features) and how the Audience will benefit from your service in such a way as to remove every single speed bump/question on the purchasing-decision-road which we are leading them down.

So much so that, by the time we reach the end of that road, they will have had all their questions answered and will be left in such a state of mind as to think "there is no good reason why I should not go ahead with this."

In summary, contrary to what you may have been told, the marketing message is not designed to nudge anyone into make a buying decision, but rather to engage an ideal client into wanting to know more.

And even though we want to pack that marketing message with words that have our Audience feeling (there's that word again) motivated to want to know more, it will never be enough on its own. That's because the marketing process may start with an emotion, but the rest of the process involves the rational and logical explanation of why your service is the very best choice for your ideal clients.

Having said that, your marketing message/USP is not enough for people to instantly wanted to buy, but it does have to be good enough to achieve the twin objectives of getting the cut-through necessary to gain the attention of your ideal client, and then motivating them to want to take the next step.

The next step may be to read an email.

The next step may be to register for a webinar.

The next step may be to have them click on your book to see inside it when surfing Amazon.

The next step may be for them to attend the event that they previously registered for.

The next step may be for them to book a time to speak with you to validate that your service is a fit for their needs.

In that sense, you can see that our marketing process consists of an initial marketing message and then a series of smaller marketing messages each of which, in turn, continues to create cut-through and capture the attention of our ideal client and then motivate them to go to the next step.

In my last book, I referred to this as the Bait Trail and I used the analogy of Hansel and Gretel being led to the wicked witch by a series of lollies that were sprinkled on the pathway through the forest that led to her house.

It's a pretty useful way to illustrate the fact that a marketing process consists of a series of steps, and that at each and every step we need to capture the attention of the Audience and motivate them to take the next step.

The three characteristics of most effective marketing messages include:

1. They are benefit-rich

2. They contain specifics

3. They are differentiated

(Note that item 2 above is sometimes absent from marketing message that still retain effectiveness. But where possible, specifics will improve the ability of a message to achieve cut-through.

The big mistake that almost everyone makes is to describe their product or service in their marketing message.

For example, an international bedding manufacturer has the following marketing message/USP:

"Better beds"

That's a classic example of a quality manufacturer that's chosen to feature their product in their marketing message as opposed to the benefit of their product (see characteristic number one above).

What would instantly improve their advertising results would be to change their marketing message to the following:

"A better sleep"

Or better still…

"A better sleep – guaranteed, or your money back"

People don't want a better bed, they want what a better bed will give them, which is a better sleep.

Or, if I wanted to be more precise, I could say that people only buy a better bed to get what they want, which is a better sleep.

Most large international companies make an absolute hash of the USP/marketing message.

Consider the $26 billion company SAP's marketing message that flashed on my television screen just yesterday:

"SAP. Run Simple."

What?

Is this an advertisement for running shoes?

I'm guessing there was an advertising agency somewhere, that got paid maybe $1 million to run a whole bunch of focus groups and then run a competition of some sort and then have several committee meetings which ultimately produced that marketing message.

Only the people in the room at the time of the final decision would have any idea of what the heck the message means, and certainly no one else would have any idea of what their differentiator is.

Same deal for Renault which for some reason decided that there USP will be:

"Passion for life"

Again, what the heck were these people thinking?

Where is the differentiation?

Does it mean that Renault has a passion for life? That they want to attract people who have a passion for life?

I really have no idea. It's not like Renault has a corner on the concept of passion.

In my estimation, virtually all of the 6.2 billion people on planet Earth are very passionate about staying alive, and that being the case, they would be more inclined to not drive a car at all.

I do not know what Mr. and Mrs. Renault were smoking when they came up with their marketing message, but whatever it was it didn't help.

Having a great marketing message is probably a heck of a lot easier for you to create as the owner of the business than it is for a giant multinational. But just to prove that it is possible, consider some of excellent corporate marketing messages that tick the boxes for what makes up a great statement.

FedEx: When it absolutely positively has to be there overnight

Benefit-rich? Check.

Contains specifics? You betcha.

Differentiated? Absolutely positively!

Or M&Ms:

"The milk chocolate that melts in your mouth, not in your hand"

Or the original Domino's Pizza marketing message:

"Delivered hot in 30 minutes, or you don't pay."

And a local example of a very small company that sat down, used common sense and came up with something that really hits the sweet spot in terms of meeting a specific unmet need for domestic electricians:

"Laser electrical: totally dependable"

And about five minutes ago, I literally just saw Microsoft's advertisement for its new Surface Pro featuring the message:

"Beautifully Powerful"

Which was previously:

"Ultra-light and versatile"

Both of which are a vast improvement on the previous version:

"From the world's number one technology company"

It's just a matter of sitting down and figuring out what your ideal clients need to hear or read that will to pique their interest.

Then make sure it's differentiated and ideally, that it contains specifics, and you got yourself a winner.

Maybe.

You still need to test it and there are five levels to that testing process which I'll share in a few pages time.

My experience is that when an organization, big or small, follows my formula for marketing messages, their sales increases are not only swift but also automatic and require no additional resource in the form of additional money, time or effort.

Think about this: by simply changing a handful of words, every business on the planet that is actively marketing can potentially improve their results significantly and swiftly.

To me, that borders on the miraculous.

Consider also this idea: let's say you find a typo in this book. A spelling error or whatever.

If you put a magnifying glass over that mistake, all that is going to happen is that you're going to see the same mistake, only bigger.

Now think about one of those big international conglomerates that seriously stuffed up their marketing message/USP.

They can throw an extra $10 million into their advertising campaigns, but at best all they are doing is magnifying their mistake and thereby making a bigger. They'll get the same lousy results, only exponentially greater.

The good news about this is that all you need to do is follow my simple formula, test your results in the manner I'm about to describe, spend virtually no money on advertising or marketing (also in the manner that I'm going to cover in Part Four) and you will be running rings around every single one of those corporate committees who have failed to look at their marketing message from a customer-centric point of view.

Hopefully, the above examples will help you to avoid the trap of describing what it is you offer, as opposed to the benefits of what you are offering.

But before I talk about testing, here's a classic and very recent example of how an international entrepreneur secured a massive deal through an effective marketing message.

Because of a very aggressive push for renewable energy sources, the South Australian government had a problem in 2016 because their mainstream electricity grid failed under a massive load during a heat wave.

The resultant power failure crippled the state, lives were lost, and political heads were about to roll.

The government decided that it needed a renewable backup supply of electricity, so they called for tenders internationally.

Some 250 tenders were submitted, but Elon Musk, who is a lover of all things renewable, met with the South Australian government and subsequently held a press conference to announce that he was offering to build the world's largest solar battery of 100MW within 100 days, or it would be free.

Pure genius.

Look at his marketing message and check it to see if it fulfilled those two objectives of being able to create cut through and motivate the prospect to want to know more.

My freaking oath it did!

Musk's marketing message made national headlines in all the major Australian papers, and most of them published his marketing message on the front page.

I doubt that there was a man, woman, child, dingo, koala or snake living in South Australia who wasn't aware of his offer.

Now let's have a look at the three characteristics of an effective marketing message and see how well he nailed them.

1. **Benefit rich**: this does not always have to be explicitly stated e.g. "a 100 MW solar and battery system", which is what he promised, is not a direct benefit but it is certainly a significantly impressive feature, being the largest solar battery in the world, which implies the benefit of continuous power supply in the event of a grid shutdown.

   This is a crucial point because it highlights that every rule has an exception and demonstrates that when a benefit is so strongly and obviously implied, you don't always have to explicitly stated. But remember: this is an exception, not the rule!

2. **Contains specifics**: 100MW and 100 days are very specific. The thing that fascinates me about specifics is that when they are pitched at the right level, they increase both believability and desirability. If Musk had promised to deliver in just 10 days, it may have well been desirable, but it certainly would not have been believable. Finding the middle path in your specifics, between believability and desirability is very important.

3. **Is differentiated**: Musk was the only one that I am aware of out of 250 tenderers who crafted such a differentiated marketing message.

Without doubt, Musk backed up his promise with plans.

And that's a good example of what I was writing about before regarding how the marketing message begins the clients journey of discovery by getting cut-through and opening the mind of your ideal clients, but that the rest of the journey down the road toward purchasing needs to be such that all the speed bumps are removed by a rational and logical exclamation of "how it all works." Hence the critical importance of Musk's plan.

The South Australian government was not going to sign a deal with Elon Musk simply on the basis of a promise, amazing entrepreneur and businessman though he is.

Consultants will tell you to "never confuse promise with delivery." And governments and corporations alike have been burned by consultants who developed a terrific marketing message but unfortunately couldn't match it when it came time to deliver on that promise.

So yes, of course Elon Musk had to demonstrate how he was going to deliver within a hundred days.

Nevertheless, when you think about the objective of the marketing message, which was to get cut-through and motivate the ideal client (in this case the South Australian government) to go to the next step (to consider his proposal and effectively put it ahead of the other 249 tenders), it worked quite well.

To further bring to life the power of the above three characteristics and help you begin forming your own effective marketing message, let's have a look at a real-life client example.

Max started a business that develops and markets point-of-sale software for Quick Service Restaurants, or QSRs as they are known in that industry.

His clients include some of the biggest fast-food franchise chains in the world.

Before we started working together, Max's marketing message when something like this:

"We develop world-class software for QSRs"

After we applied the three characteristics, this is what his new marketing message looks like:

"We increase the sales and profits in QSRs by 25 percent or more within 90 days"

Remember our twin objectives in creating an effective marketing message are to first gain the attention of our ideal clients (getting cut-through) and second to motivate those same people to take the next step.

If Max was promoting a "lunch-and-learn" type presentation for prospective clients, you can see how much more powerful a variation of the second statement would be as a title for his presentation?

For example:

How to Increase the Sales in Your QSRs by 25 percent or More in 90 Days

Plus: how to avoid the four most common but costly point-of-sale mistakes that most QSRs make

Similarly, that title would work well on a landing page offering QSR owners a special report/guide, and it would work well as a title of the webinar. A variation of that may work well as the title of a free online diagnostic tool, or another quiz or a survey or a boardroom briefing or a conference talk, and so on.

I often say to new clients that creating a marketing message will be the most difficult part of the entire lead-generation system development process.

That's because we can't simply pump out a statement that describes what we do.

We must put ourselves into the minds and hearts of our marketplace and figure out what their specific unmet need is, reverse-engineer it so we speak to that need in a benefit-rich way, and then articulate the whole thing in such a way that it is differentiated to the point where it gets the cut-through we need.

The fact that crafting a marketing message can be hard work is the bad news.

The good news is that once we've nailed it, we can re-purpose it, as alluded to above, across multiple lead-generation assets and broadcast it into a never-ending series of audiences.

That is, at least until we decide to improve it further!

THE CONCEPT OF A MARKETING MESSAGE DOESN'T STOP WITH THE SHORT PITHY SLOGAN.

It starts there, but then we cascade it down to the rest of your marketing assets and drive the perception of you being more differentiated and more desirable deeper into the mind of your audience.

Every time someone sees your brand, I'd like them to see differentiation.

On that note, as the head of your own business, one of the worst sins that you will ever commit is to fail to promote yourself as a part of your marketing.

The greatest competitive advantage that you have against all your competitors, direct and indirect, local and global, big and small is ...

... You

There are at least three reasons for this.

First, as human beings we are wired to want social connections. Just ask Mark Zuckerberg, founder of Facebook.

Given that your ideal client is wired to want to create a relationship with another person, as opposed to an organization, you would do well to optimize the effectiveness of your marketing efforts by putting a magnifying glass in front of your personality, values, vision, beliefs, likes, and dislikes.

I'm not talking about being overtly religious or political.

I am talking about using almost every other aspect of what makes you unique in your marketing by expressing your thoughts and feelings through blogs, podcasts, interviews, articles, books, presentations, pitches, and whatever else you are doing during the course of your marketing, your value delivery to clients, and through your interactions with your team members and suppliers.

This not only makes for effective marketing, it is also what brings effective culture to life in organizations, big and small.

The second reason is that none of your competitors can compete with you, the human being, because there is only one of you.

And in the same way that your DNA and your fingerprint are unique, so too are your combined set of values, beliefs, personality, and character.

So, given that it's literally impossible for your competitors to compete on a level playing field with you, the individual, let's milk that advantage for all it's worth!

The third reason may possibly be regarded as more esoteric, but in fact I view it as far more practical than either of the above two.

You are in possession of a gift and your purpose is to give that gift to the world.

Not the whole world, just your part of it.

As mentioned, your gift is a part of you and therefore it is equally unique.

But if you set up a website that looks like a bank's website, or if you speak like you've been trained using a someone else's formula instead of your own voice, and if you write as if it's a letter to the Queen, you are effectively "hiding your light under a bushel," as they say.

In short, I don't believe that you can fulfill your potential or your purpose in life by trying to be someone you're not.

I therefore want you to regard these words as your permission slip to be the you that you were born to be.

Demonstrate passion about what you believe is right within your industry, demonstrate passion about what you believe is wrong within your industry, stand up and be counted, let your voice be heard, and you may be surprised how much that authenticity will add to the power of your brand.

(Just make sure that the demonstration of your passion is relevant to your market and don't make the mistake of believing that your passion alone will be enough to generate new clients.

Fashion is an important ingredient in the recipe, but it's not the whole recipe.)

VALIDATING A MARKETING MESSAGE WITH MY FIVE-STAGE TESTING PROCESS

A long time ago, I learned never to trust what a client thought their Audience wanted to hear.

And soon after, I learned never to trust myself to know what my client's Audience wanted to hear.

The bottom line here is that marketing messages must be tested, as opposed to us simply sitting in our ivory towers and having a thought bubble up that we've got a world-beating winner, which in my experience is something that generally occurs somewhere between the first and second bottle of wine.

Before you test, you will, ideally, come up with three variations of what you think would be a great marketing message, and ensure that the variations are significant within each message.

For example, if I was starting again, I might come up with the following three variations:

A. Get more clients, get more revenue, have more fun.

B. Enjoy a weekly flow of inbound, new client inquiries.

C. Wake up every Monday morning to calendar bookings from people eager to talk with you about becoming a client.

Having come up with three variations of your own, you can then follow the following five steps to make sure that your marketing message is going to get the cut through that you're aiming for, as well as get an ideal client motivated to want to know more.

1. THE THREE-TICK TEST

The first thing to do is to ask yourself whether you can put a tick next to each statement when you ask the following three questions:

A. Can I *deliver* on the promise inherent in the statement?

B. Is the promise inherent in the statement highly *desirable*?

C. Is the promise inherent in the statement *believable*?

For example, my client, Susan, in Canada, can improve measurable productivity in an organization by 50 percent in less than 12 months.

And while she can deliver that sort of transformation, and while it's highly desirable for her client companies, "50 percent in 12 months" are not numbers which most senior decision-makers would find believable.

Similarly, my client, Frank, in Philadelphia, has a 100 percent success rate for his Big Data and AI software development work. The problem is that the industry has an estimated 34 percent completion rate and people who haven't worked with Frank yet don't believe that he can deliver on the 100 percent figure. So we had to dumb it down to 97 percent.

If the thing is believable but not desirable, no one is going to buy.

And when a thing is desirable but not believable, people will be inclined to assume that the seller is a just another BS artist or hype-merchant.

It's therefore always a matter of finding the middle ground between desirability and believability.

2. THE DINNER PARTY TEST

Go and sit in your imaginary "common sense corner," take a few deep breaths to clear your mind, and then imagine yourself at a dinner party sitting next to a prospective ideal client.

This person has downed a few glasses of wine and for some reason is pouring their heart out about their problems, challenges, and opportunities.

And as luck would have it, they are describing the exact situation that you could help them with.

Eventually their verbal outpouring ceases, they put the glass down, and they say to you: "I'm sorry, I've been very rude telling you all about my issues. Tell me, what is it that you do for a living?"

Then imagine yourself responding with the first of the three marketing messages that you drafted.

And still sitting on your common-sense corner, imagine what their response would be.

Would their eyes widen and would they lean forward and ask: "That sounds interesting, how do you do that?"

Or, would they smile weakly, say something like "that's nice" and turn to the person on the other side and introduced themselves?

If, in your mind, you experience the former scenario, then move onto the next question, and once you've got an imaginary positive response for each of the three statements, you're ready to go to the next step.

3. THE IDEAL CLIENT TEST

Make a list of 15 people who represent your ideal clients. They can be past clients, present clients, and even potential future clients.

You must know these people well enough so that, if you call them on their mobile phone, and they could see it was you calling, they would pick up and be happy to hear from you.

Then you email each of those 15 people asking for a favor. You explain to them that you're conducting a marketing exercise and that you need responses from people in your marketplace you respect and trust.

Go on to explain that you simply need them to click reply and let you know "which one of the following three statements would most motivate them to want to know more."

Let them know that, while you welcome suggestions and alternatives, you really need them to just pick one.

Given that you've approached 15 people, on average you'll find that 10 people respond quite swiftly.

Of those 10, you should expect 6 or more to pick the same statement. If you achieve that threshold, then you've got yourself a winner and you can go on to the next test.

If you don't achieve that passing mark, then it's back to step one.

I know that going back to step one can be a pain in the butt; but it's like I said before, if you magnify a mistake, you only get a bigger mistake.

And if you don't get your marketing message right, then all the hard work and effort you put into building your assets and finding the audiences again may come to nothing.

I'm an absolute stickler for nailing the marketing message. I've had some clients who come up with a message in less than 30 minutes that's then been validated by the marketplace, and we're good to go.

But if it takes three months to achieve the same result, then so be it.

Think of it as akin to laying down the foundation for a new house. If it's not as solid as a rock, then everything you build on top of it will simply fall down around your ears.

It's better to take the pain up front and enjoy the rewards later, than to be sloppy up front and have the pain later.

4. THE MARKETPLACE TEST

Once you've got your winner confirmed in the previous step, then the time has come to confirm that your message will work in the real world of commercial enterprise.

To do this, you embed that marketing message into your marketing assets and observe the results.

In tennis, I get to find out whether the technique that I've been practicing on the practice court works only when I play a competition match and the points are being scored. Until then, it's too easy to fool myself into thinking that I've mastered the technique.

And it's the same in business; until you start converting prospects to inquiries at a greater rate than previously, you don't know for sure whether your new marketing message is a winner.

5. THE BANK BALANCE TEST

Following the same theme of validating your marketing message, there is no validation greater than seeing more money flow into your bank account as a result of your marketing efforts.

And that's always the ultimate and final test.

OTHER WAYS TO CASCADE YOUR MESSAGE OUT INTO THE MARKET

In addition to using your personality to build relationships of "know, like, and trust" with your ideal clients as a prequel to working with them, there are other ways to drive the perception of differentiation and desirability even deeper.

The first thing I recommend you do is come up with a name for what it is you do.

For example, I don't offer "marketing" or "lead generation."

You probably think that I do, and I can understand why, because I use those phrases a fair bit.

But when you think about it, a more commonly recurring theme throughout this book is the word "Leadsology.®"

And please note the little registered logo at the end of that word.

Leadsology® is a word that I invented to describe the science of generating inbound leads (refer to the forest full of bears and my honey pots mentioned in the Preface).

Right now, metaphorically speaking, the chances are that your marketplace perceives you to be in the middle of a continent, amongst hundreds or thousands of competitors, and that you all have your hands up and are shouting "pick me!"

But when you come up with a proprietary name for your service, and you register it, then you make it not only unique but legally protected. It's like you just moved yourself to an island off the coast of the continent that only you occupy.

You've left all your competitors behind on the mainland.

And for one of your ideal clients to engage your services, they must come to your island.

There are probably half a million people or more around the world who will tell you that they can help you with your marketing.

I have no idea what the number is but it's certainly a very big one.

I'm the only game in town though, if you want Leadsology.®

And when I reinforce the uniqueness of my brand by telling a potential new client that they don't have to pay any money up front, the desirability of the brand increases further still.

Everything you can do that drives the idea that you offer desirable differentiation is worth pursuing and nothing makes that differentiation more obvious than a registered proprietary brand-name.

It may well be that the vast majority of your prospective ideal clients don't know that what you've got is significantly different and significantly better than that of your competitors.

In that regard, we both share the same problem: How the heck do we quite rightly shift the marketplace's perception from the idea that what we offer is similar to our competitors, to the idea that what we offer is both different and more desirable?

It's easy to do that with word-of-mouth marketing.

For example, a client of yours who loves your work, meets for coffee with a friend who shares a problem, and your client tells the friend that you can help them with their problem and refers them to you.

Converting a prospect like that is a piece of cake.

Almost always, the referred person meets with you having already decided they want to work with you, even before you open your mouth.

But what about the other 99.999 percent of your potential marketplace who don't know that you even exist?

How are you going to convince them that what you've got is different and better?

I've already answered the question of how you get their attention (see the three characteristics of effective marketing messages above), but to shift the perception of your ideal clients to more accurately see that you are differentiated, you can come up with a proprietary name, register it as a trademark, and then market the heck out of it.

For example, a client of mine, Peter, in Sydney Australia, specializes in increasing sales by getting the marketing and sales divisions of large organizations working together (as opposed to what they famously do, which is to fight like cats and dogs).

Peter has registered Smarketing® here in Australia. If you fall in love with the idea of Smarketing® and your business operates in Australia, then Peter is the only game in town.

Another client, Paul, in the UK, who finds tech companies that can be acquired by larger non-tech companies, flew out to Australia for a day to meet with me and we came up with the name Techquisition,® which he has since registered in both the European Union and United States, his two major markets.

I'm not a trademark attorney and I'm not about to offer you specific advice on what you can and cannot register as a trademark, but I am prepared to give you a couple of general tips in the interests of getting you started.

Of course, you should consult a trademark attorney or your local government agency to confirm that you have something that you can register as a trademark.

A BRIEF INTRODUCTION TO WHAT YOU CAN REGISTER AS A TRADEMARK

For every trademark that you register, you must prove that it's distinctive from your competitors.

Trademarks can be registered by industry category, so you don't have to come up with something that is 100 percent unique across all industries.

Furthermore, you can register a trademark in your country alone. Someone else might have the same word or phrase registered in another country or for another industry, but that doesn't stop you from registering your own trademark in your country of business.

If you want to find out if a trademark has already been claimed in your industry or your country, you can go to the world intellectual property organization global brand database at **www. wipo.int/branddb/** and check it out.

A trademark will cost you anywhere between $400 and $600 to register in most countries, and if you want to register the trademark in more than one country, you're probably best to do it first in the country where your business is registered.

Your options are to either find a trademark attorney and discuss with them your options, or to go and find your federal government's IP (intellectual property) website and applied directly for you trademark.

The advantages of going through trademark attorney is that you can save time and money by avoiding the rejection process.

Trademark attorneys typically are relatively inexpensive and they can make the process of registering a trademark much easier and faster. In addition, they can save you money by avoiding rejections from the government agency because you don't have something that can be registered as a trademark.

Either way, once you've got a registered trademark in the country where you do business, you will be issued a unique trademark registration number and you can then apply for expanding your trademark protection into other countries through a system called the Madrid Protocol, which allows you to file one application for up to 191 different countries using just the one application.

In most countries, you can use your government's IP website as a portal through which to apply for international trademark registrations.

If that's not the case in the country that you're doing business in, you can go direct to **www.wipo.int**.

REGISTERING A WORD AS A TRADEMARK

To oversimplify the concept of trademarks, there are essentially two items that you can register: One is a word or phrase, and the other is an image.

It's very unlikely that you will be able to use words that are in common use.

For example, if I tried to register "ClickMarketing," then my application would get knocked back because there is nothing distinctive about the new word, since it was created by pushing two existing words together.

I was able to register Leadsology® because it's not a word that's in common use and neither is it simply mashing two common words together.

To illustrate that point, I wouldn't be able to register the name "LeadStream," but I can register "Leadsology LeadStream®" because the inclusion of the first word in that phrase makes the phrase in its entirety differentiated.

REGISTERING AN IMAGE AS A TRADEMARK

This is infinitely easier because you can create a stylized image such as a cartoon character or a unique way of presenting a word or phrase.

For example, one brand incorporates the shapes of rabbit, duck, and giraffe to make up the word "Kidsafe".

The owner of that image can't register the word "Kidsafe," but they can register the image described above because it's distinctive and unique.

Naturally, there's a whole lot more to the ins and outs of registering a trademark than I have neither the time, the inclination, nor the ability to comment on, but that should be enough to get you started.

On a local note, the Australian government offers an outstanding and completely customized service including being very proactive in calling applicants to discuss their applications.

In almost all other countries, I've had a trademark accepted through the World Intellectual Property Organization's website at **www.wipo.int**.

The one exception was getting the trademark registered in the USA, and I needed to hire a USA-based attorney for that.

I was very fortunate to be introduced to Nicholas D Wells of the Legends Law Group based in Kaysville, Utah, who can be found at **www.Legendslaw.com**.

Nicholas deserves a worthy mention here, not only because he sent me a personalized direct mail letter all the way from Utah to Castaways Beach here in Australia offering services for a fixed fee (which he honored), but also because he completed the application on my behalf seamlessly and swiftly.

YOU SHOULD BE VERY PROACTIVE AND VERY OVERT ABOUT YOUR DIFFERENTIATION

I was presenting to an audience this morning about the subject of differentiation. The audience consisted almost entirely of consultants, corporate trainers, and executive/business coaches.

I explained to them that people judge a book by its cover.

I asked them if we should judge a book by its cover and they responded adamantly that no, we should not.

We all agreed that, in fact, a book should be judged by its content, not its cover.

But imagine standing alongside a prospective client in front of a bookshelf that contained 1,000 books on the subject of your area of expertise.

And you can spot your book among all the other books on that bookshelf.

And you know that your prospective client is looking for a book on the subject of your expertise and, like you, they can see 1,000 books on that subject in front of them on the bookshelf.

You also know that the content of your book is so differentiated and so much better than the other 999 that it will most certainly be the best choice for the person standing next to you.

You hope they pick your book.

You watch them as they scan row after row of the books in front of them, but their eyes never seem to come to rest on your book.

Dang!

Why not?

Because every single one of the 1,000 books have identical words on the cover.

And for most people who are Marketing The Invisible, that analogy is a pretty darned accurate one, because it depicts the reality of what a prospective ideal client experiences when seeking a supplier.

For example, go to almost any single business coach's' website on the planet and you'll find words like

- We help you grow business
- We show you how to increase sales
- We show you how to earn more in less time
- Variations of the above themes

If the words you use to describe your service are similar to the words used by your competitors on their websites, on their business cards, in their promotional assets, on their LinkedIn profile, on the landing pages, and so on… then you are that proverbial book hidden amongst all the other books and it's no wonder no one is picking it up.

Here in Australia, if someone goes to buy a packet of cigarettes, they'll noticed that every single packet has a cover that's identical to every other packet.

You literally cannot tell the difference between the contents of one cigarette packet and another.

That's because the government introduced legislation to stop tobacco companies from advertising either in the media or through sponsorships, signage, and even on the cover of their own cigarette packets.

In other words, each tobacco company has been forced through government legislation to make their "book cover" look the same as their competitors.

Professionals are bound by no such regulation, and yet it's extraordinary how they engage in the same practice of what I call "Plain Package Marketing."

In fact, I'd argue that's not marketing at all. Rather, it's what we might call "name, rank, and serial number" information.

What am I saying here?

I'm paraphrasing Coco Chanel and saying, *"In order to be in demand one must be both differentiated and desirable."*

That starts with your marketing message and continues as you express your personality, ideas, and values in your marketing, and it runs even deeper when you register a proprietary term to describe your service. It's reinforced even more when you choose to use proprietary graphics and unique ways to explain to clients what it is that you do and how you do it.

EIGHT REASONS WHY

One of the toughest exercises that I have my clients complete is to come up with eight clearly stated reasons why their prospective client should consider them to be their number one choice.

When you think about it, this is an exercise that everyone should complete prior to launching a business, and it therefore surprises me how few people undertake it.

Admittedly, when you first try this exercise, it may make your brain hurt.

In addition to coming up with eight clear reasons, including specifics, I give my clients very little "real estate" to write out their reasons.

Mark Twain apparently once started a letter with the words "I'm sorry this is going to be such a long letter, but I simply don't have enough time to make it a shorter one."

When we are forced to make a thing succinct, we must distill the essence of what we want to say by following William Faulkner's advice to "kill your darlings" (which he apparently paraphrased from Arthur Quiller-Couch, who advised writers to "murder your darlings").

The Eight Reasons Why exercise forces you to come up with a powerful list of reasons that clearly and directly communicates to your prospective clients why you are significantly differentiated and more desirable than any of your competitors.

In marketing, we call this "making the invisible, visible."

Following is an example of Eight Reasons Why written by my client, Frank, in Philadelphia, who owns the company specializing in Big Data and Artificial Intelligence programming skills.

To understand how powerful these eight reasons are in Frank's marketplace, remember that most AI projects never get completed, and those that are completed mostly don't get used by the intended team they were built for.

Further, most of Frank's competitors go over budget and fail to deliver on time.

You can imagine therefore, some of the frustrations that Frank's ideal clients will have experienced in the past.

And while Frank's services have always been exceptional, we need to "make the invisible visible."

Here are Frank's Eight Reasons Why:

1. We can evidence a 97 percent success rate.

2. We deliver each agreed project milestone on time and, if we ever fail to, then you don't have to pay that month's invoice.

3. We never, ever blow budget.

4. We're fussy about who we work with. On average we turn down two out of three job requests. That's because we only take on projects that we can get over the line.

5. We make sure that your team can, will, and do use the system effectively once we're gone, because we train them, support them with systems to follow and we coach them based on their experience and feedback.

6. Not only that, we empower your team to the point where you are in control of the system once we're gone, and you can continue to monitor, refine, and update.

7. We operate a 7-point Communication Charter to ensure clear and consistent communication so that you feel in control during the project, and so that you know what's

going on and where we're at in real time 24/7 using our exclusive chat portal.

8. We have a 5-point Team Integration Protocol (TIP) to ensure we work as seamlessly as possible with your own IT team.

In particular I'd like you to note what a great job Frank has done of including specifics in many of his reasons.

For example, instead of saying something like "we give great Customer Service," he's talked about a seven-point communication charter, a 24/7 chat portal, a five-point Team Integration Protocol, and so on.

The problem with simply using generalized statements such as "great customer service" is that anyone can, and invariably does, say the same thing. And that means you're sitting back there in the middle of 999 other books, with the same thing printed on every cover.

By including specifics in your marketing, you increase differentiation, but you also strengthen both credibility and desirability.

DIFFERENTIATION VIA VALUE DELIVERY MODELS

A final note on your marketing message.

I see website after website saying...

- We are passionate about...
- Here is our vision and mission statement and our values...
- Here's our team...
- Here's is a list of our services...

- Here's my blog that talks even more about me...

- Here's my photo in my job title...

Unfortunately, no one gives a rat's tush about that stuff other than the person who wrote it.

The fundamental truth of being a human being is that each individual lives and feels as if they are the center of the universe.

They do not, I repeat, they do not, live and feel as if *you* are the center of the universe.

Marketing is about giving people what they want and, if they have any inkling of interest in your services, then they will want to know more about how you can help them.

For the purpose of making a point, I'm focusing on websites, but the same point applies to business cards or LinkedIn profiles or any other point of contact where prospective clients are going to be checking you out.

To that end, I urge you to make your marketing market-centric, not ego-centric.

The Assets

Strategic Question #4: What's The Way To Get The MESSAGE About My MAGIC In Front Of My AUDIENCE?

I HAVE GOOD NEWS and bad news.

The bad news is that you can't dabble in marketing.

It's one of those things that just doesn't work if you try it in a half-hearted manner.

Unfortunately, most people want the one marketing tip that gets them new clients easily, simply, effortlessly, fast and preferably at zero cost.

The newsflash for those people is that it doesn't exist and the evidence that it doesn't exist is the fact that I'm still in business.

Some people have told me that all their marketing problems are over because they just bought a great list.

They don't realize that buying a list or identifying a prospect is one of the easiest things in the world and that the hard part is leading those prospects through the four levels of Psychological Allure including Rapport, Respect, Relatability and Reciprocity (more on that in part four).

To walk a prospect through the journey from their opening position of not having heard of you, to being justifiably skeptical and eventually to a place where they hope like heck that you accept them as a client, needs what I call "real estate."

In other words, we need some time with them to lead them down the road of discovering and validating that your services are their best option.

And that real estate is what I call your marketing Assets.

In life, there are the haves and the have-nots.

The haves have what they want, and the have-nots don't have what they want.

For those Marketing The Invisible, the great separating characteristic between the haves and the have-nots are marketing Assets.

The haves take the time and trouble to develop marketing Assets because they know that it not only makes their marketing more effective, it makes their marketing more efficient as well.

The biggest Asset that the have-nots have is a business card.

People complain that "today's generation" are into instant gratification.

I'm willing to bet that complaint has been expressed for thousands of years.

So, I'm not going be one of those people who moan and groan about "young people today."

But I will be the guy who points out what you already know, which is that you need to sacrifice time and energy and maybe a little less money in the short term (take the pain up front) in order to get what you want in the medium to long term.

It's like you have a choice: Do you want to put up a tent or build a house?

This metaphor comes from a remarkably talented graphic designer by the name of Tatiana.

Tatiana lives locally and asked if I'd meet her for a coffee to discuss her business and whether I could help.

I will almost always have a coffee with someone who asks, with the possible caveat that I'll name the cafe to make sure I get a decent espresso.

Anyhow, back to Tatiana.

I listened as she told me about her business and what she had tried in regard to marketing and how it had worked for her.

That part of our meeting was a fairly short conversation.

Because she pretty much relied on word-of-mouth marketing plus a local business networking meeting for new clients.

Naturally, she asked what I'd recommend in the way of setting up effective lead generation systems.

I explained the concept of Assets and Audiences, Monty and the beehives (I'll cover this one shortly) and so on.

"Wow" she said. "Creating those Assets sounds like a lot of work."

I replied that yes, it was.

But I then asked her a question: "Tatiana how long have you been running your current business?"

"17 years," she replied.

"Well," I said, "in a marketing sense, it's been like you've been living in a tent for 17 years."

Can you survive in a tent?

Yes, you certainly can.

But hygiene can be a bit of an issue and it gets pretty cold in the winter and quite uncomfortable in the summer and, frankly, there's not much of a lifestyle; it's more a matter of surviving.

But if you would like to work with me, we can build you a house.

And yes, it's a lot of work.

But consider this: Once the house is built, you get to enjoy a much higher quality of lifestyle and a level of comfort that you can continue enjoying for decades to come.

And that would never have been possible had you chosen to stay living in the tent.

And it's the same with marketing Assets.

If you are prepared to sacrifice some time and some effort, and a relatively small amount of money in the short term, to build the right Assets, and build the Assets right (two separate things), then the quality of your life will improve exponentially, and you'll shift from surviving in your business to thriving in your business.

Note the two caveats I offered: The right Assets built the right way.

For example, almost anyone can write a book.

I was a guy who got held back from starting school because I couldn't put a sentence together. I also had to repeat the last year of high school, which I managed to fail two years in a row. That means I'm not exactly Einstein. It also means that if I can write a bestseller, then the chances are that you can to.

In fact, this is my fourth book.

The first one generated almost 0 new clients.

The second one generated a couple of clients.

The third one generated a lot of clients.

And knowing what I know now about how to generate clients from the book, I'd suggest that this one will generate even more clients.

The difference between my first book and this book is that before I knew that I was building the right asset, and now I know how to build the asset right.

And I'll reveal more when we dive into the Leadsology® Persuasion Sequence.

It's the same with other assets, including webinars or seminars or surveys or e-guides: Each Asset has to be the right one for your Audience and it has to be built in such a way that it leads your Audience gently but firmly to the conclusion that you are their best, if not their only, option for helping to solve the problems and/or meet the challenges and/or fulfill the potential of their opportunity.

That said, here's an initial list of just some of the Assets that you can develop:

1. Printed or downloadable Guide/Report
2. Seminar/workshop presentation
3. Conference speaking presentation
4. Webinar
5. Book
6. Challenge
7. Boardroom Briefing
8. Online Funnel
9. Interactive Model
10. Enrollment/Application page
11. Survey
12. Diagnostic
13. Closed Facebook Group
14. LinkedIn group
15. Articles

16. Blog
17. Podcast host
18. Podcast guest
19. Boot Camp on-line
20. Masterclass off-line
21. Consult
22. Trial
23. Website
24. Landing pages
25. Autoresponders sequence (a.k.a. indoctrination series)

Note that the above list refers to marketing Assets, as opposed to infrastructure Assets, the latter being the behind-the-scenes Assets such as an online booking scheduler that allows your prospects to find a time to talk with you about becoming a client, an email database, an online meeting room such as **www.zoom.us** or **www.gotomeeting.com** and other infrastructure Assets.

You find a list some of the assets that I use and recommend under the Essential Infrastructure Assets bonus chapter at the end of this book.

The specific marketing Assets you should develop will depend on the type of Audience you are targeting.

By way of illustration, allow me to indulge in another analogy.

I'm fortunate to live in park-like grounds on the sand next to the beach. Our house and swimming pool is surrounded with palm trees and other native Australian trees along with bamboo and lots of flowers, and so it is more like a small park than a backyard.

I also have four bee hives nestled amongst the trees and flowers.

And as you know by now, I have my erstwhile companion, Monty the Marketing Wonder Dog (my Border Collie friend) whose dinner bowl sits in our backyard not too far from the bee hives.

Right now, in the house, I have a bunch of flowers and I have some steak in the fridge.

If I were to grab the flowers and walk out to the back yard with Monty and place the bunch of flowers in his dinner bowl, he'd take one look at the flowers and then look up at me with those puppy dog eyes, cocking his head to one side, picking up his ears before asking me if I'd lost my marbles.

Similarly, if I were to take the steak from the fridge and put it on a plate in front of one of our beehives, the bees would be equally nonplussed about the steak as Monty was about the flowers.

Back to Monty.

For me to get Monty to eat the flowers would require the equivalent of a lot of hard selling.

And that's what it's like when you put the wrong Asset in front of the right Audience.

It's a flop.

But imagine I swap those two "Assets" around and put the steak in Monty's dinner bowl and the flowers in front of the beehive.

How much selling would I need to do at that point?

Of course, the answer is absolutely none.

Why?

Because I matched the Asset to the Audience.

And that's what good marketing does.

When we match the right Asset to the right Audience, there is zero selling required.

When you put the right asset in front of the right Audience, people consume it almost as fast as Monty eats a steak.

To further illustrate the point, if you are marketing to the CEOs of some of the world's largest corporations, then inviting them to attend a 90-minute webinar is like trying to convince Monty that he really wants to eat the flowers. Good luck with that.

I'll give you a better idea of which Assets are suited to which Audiences in Part Three, which is coming your way soon.

In the meantime, what I recommend you do is decide to build your first Asset.

Once you read Part Three, you'll be in a much better position to figure out what that Asset should be.

But build your first Asset, get it into the marketplace, test it, fix the mistakes and get it back out into the marketplace.

After a bit of trialing and observing, that Asset will help build your list and generate new clients; probably just a trickle, but nevertheless a start.

Once you have that first Asset up and running and working well, you will have freed up some more time to go back and develop the second Asset.

Rinse and repeat the same way: Fix any mistakes and relaunch, then rinse and repeat until it's working well.

Then you'll have freed up some more time again, and so you go develop your third Asset and your fourth Asset and as many Assets as you need to fill your pipeline with the number of high-quality prospects that you need to achieve your sales objectives.

I flagged this in the preface but it's worth repeating: This is not a step-by-step training manual and it's not a coaching program and it can't take the place of private mentoring work.

However, it is a book which will clearly shine the light on the path you need to head down if you want to turn the idea of an inbound flow of new leads into reality.

And so if you want a hand with all of that journey, let me know by emailing me at **tom@leadsology.guru** or going to **www.Book-AChatWithTom.com** and find a time for us to talk.

PART THREE

CREATING SECURITY OF LEAD GENERATION AND ADDITIONAL POWER VIA LEADSOLOGY LEADSTREAMS®

Creating Security, Abundance and Fulfillment

Welcome to Leadsology Leadstreams®

By THIS STAGE, you know something about what I do to make a buck: I work with professionals who offer service, advice or software, and together we embed lead-generation systems into their businesses so that they can enjoy a high-quality flow of inbound, new client inquiries virtually every week of the year.

But if you look at the services I offer from a bigger perspective, I help professionals create better businesses, which in turn gives them the potential to create better lives for themselves and their families.

And that's important to remember when we consider the concept of Leadsology LeadStreams® and here's why.

The concept of "Multiple Streams of Income" sought to achieve a similar goal; that of improving quality of people's lives by increasing both the volume and security of income through diversification and multiplication of income streams.

In principle, the idea of Multiple Streams of Income is very sound, but as is often the case with these concepts, it was taken up by far too many people who had no idea of what they were talking about, packaged up into courses, programs, and workshops, which they then sold for a lot of money.

Notwithstanding that, anyone who wants a financially secure future, including more choice about the type of home they live in, where they live, the quality of their children's education, vacations, philanthropic pursuits, community involvement, and so on ... would do well to add fresh income streams to whatever stream they currently possess.

The diversity that is inherent in multiple streams of income not only generates the potential for more income, but also leads to increased security.

In marketing, Multiple Streams of Leads provides us with a strikingly similar result: increasing the volume of leads and increasing the security of that volume through diversification.

It still constantly surprises me how many times I hear of people who retire with a multi-million-dollar nest egg, and then get convinced by a friend or relative that they can make a big return on their investment by lending it to that friend or relative so that they can grow their business.

Invariably, after a year or two, they would settle for a return _of_ their investment and forget about any thought of a return _on_ their investment.

The scariest number in investment circles is the number one.

If you have all your money in one investment, then you are in danger of being critically vulnerable to any change, whether it's a foreign power driving tanks into a neighbor's desert and sparking an international conflict, or lenders indulging in too many sub-prime loans initiating an eight-year Global Financial Crisis, or indeed just your common garden variety business/industry collapse.

I'm aware that when it comes to investing big chunks of money, that everything that I've said above is common sense.

You know it's true, right?

So why then are you nodding your head sagely, in agreement with the wisdom of diversifying investments if you have only one current source of leads which is word-of-mouth marketing.

And chances are that even that one source of leads is beyond your direct control.

In other words, if you're depended on word-of-mouth marketing then you can't push a button or pull a lever and have leads flowing in. You must sit and wait and hope.

In reality, I don't know if that applies to you or not.

But I do know that, based on the number of people I've worked with, it does apply to 9 out of 10 professionals who have some Magic.

In Part One under "The Domino Effect," I wrote about how, if you are the primary breadwinner in your family, then your financial choices in life are completely and entirely dependent on your ability to generate new client inquiries.

Please allow me to be brutally honest: A failure to develop multiple streams of leads is a failure to fulfill both your obligations as a financial provider for your family (if you don't have a family then you can ignore that) as well as a failure to live up to the potential of your life purpose in serving a greater number of your fellow human beings with the gifts that you are given and the skills that you've developed.

And by way of further encouraging you drop the idea of dabbling in marketing, and instead to seriously commit to the development of multiple streams of leads, I'd suggest that if you're like many others, you have what I'd call "10 out of 10 Magic, trapped inside 1 out of 10 marketing."

Charlatans and fraudsters and con men/woman all have one thing in common, other than their narcissistic and commercially psychopathic mindsets: They all reverse those numbers. They have 10 out of 10 marketing wrapped around a 1 out of 10 value proposition.

Let's agree then, that as a smart/wise/astute/knowledgeable professional you need to find a way to embed multiple streams of leads into your business so that you not only generate significantly more income and enhance your lifestyle choices, but you also massively increase the security of the same, and move yourself dramatically closer to fulfilling your life purpose.

Or, did you have better plan?

THE UMBRELLA VIEW OF LEADSOLOGY LEADSTREAMS®

Each of my Leadsology LeadStreams® is made up of three elements:

Element #1: The Audience

Element #2: The Asset

Element #3: The Persuasion Sequence

Please note well that to save yourself years of disappointment and frustration, you must nail each of these three elements simultaneously so that you can enjoy a flow of new client inquiries: a stream of leads.

Having read this far, you will be very familiar with the first two elements listed above.

Regarding the third element, I'll give you a step-by-step sequence to follow in respect to The Persuasion Sequence in the next part of this book.

But what we can have a look at now is how to match the assets to the Audiences for your specific market.

BUT FIRST A WORD OF CAUTION

Naturally, I don't know exactly which market you are targeting, but it will be one of the three mentioned previously, which are the Corporate market the SMEs/solopreneur market, or the Consumer market.

And if you think that you are serving more than one market and you also think that you can develop Leadsology LeadStreams® for those markets simultaneously, allow me please to slap you hard across each cheek, virtually, and place some smelling salts under your nose so that you wake up and come back to the real world.

Unless you have access to massive funds, I would very strongly recommend that you follow my advice and "pick one" market to focus on developing Leadsology LeadStreams® for.

That's because the concept of "multiple focus" is a contradiction in terms, also known as an oxymoron.

A bit like military intelligence, open secret, larger half, alone together, and at the risk of offending Bill Gates, "Microsoft Works," which was mercifully laid to rest in 2007.

Anyhow, you get the idea: The word focus implies that we are looking at one thing, and one thing only.

Otherwise you don't get focus, you get blur, and that's the enemy of effective strategy, which demands that you pay attention to the specific unmet need of one Audience and that you address those needs with one Magic and that you generate interest in that Magic initially with one on my Leadsology LeadStreams,® get that working well, and then go back and add another, and another, and another.

LEADSOLOGY LEADSTREAMS® FOR THE SME/ SOLOPRENEUR MARKET

Let me start by letting you know what's currently proving to be the most effective Leadsology LeadStreams® for the SME/solopreneur market.

Of course, this is the market that Leadsology® serves, so I know it doubly well, not only from my point of view, but also from the point of view of showing my clients who serve this market how to embed Leadsology LeadStreams® into their business.

A CAVEAT

I'll discuss this in more detail toward the end of this part of the book, but it is worth noting in advance that in just the same way that a physical stream of water can change in direction or volume, so too can a Leadsology LeadStream.®

That means that the one I am about to present to you may change.

Nevertheless, at the time of writing, these are the Leadsology LeadStreams®, including the assets and Audiences, that are producing a regular flow of leads efficiently and effectively in the SME/solopreneur market.

(Please note that where I use the term "Consult" I'm referring to a meeting where a prospect has booked a time to speak with you to explore the idea of working together. And you can refer to Part Two if you need a refresher on the subject of Other Peoples Networks, or OPN)

Chart A

A special note for audio book listeners. in the book I present the chart which you'll find in a downloadable PDF. It's available to you as part of your purchase. I recommend that you pause the recording at this point, download the PDF of Chart A Part 6 and view the chart. Then restart the recording.

LeadStream®	Primary Asset	Best Audiences	Purpose
Webinar Typically, a one-hour training meeting with a large number of attendees	PowerPoint presentation*	1. Your own email list 2. OPN email list 3. LinkedIn	1. List building 2. Generating consults 3. Keeping your brand in the brain of your list until they are ready to buy (BBB)
Boardroom Briefings A smaller, more intimate and exclusive variation of a training webinar with much higher levels of engagement and interaction from participants including some form of Hot Seat	PowerPoint presentation*	1. Your own email list 2. OPN email list 3. LinkedIn	1. Generating consults 2. List building
Five-Day Challenge A series of daily training and action challenges typically presented through short videos and designed to give participants a taste of the transformation you offer	Training videos and training page for each day	1. OPN email list 2. Your own list (once a year)	1. List-building 2. BBB

LeadStream®	Primary Asset	Best Audiences	Purpose
Podcast Guest Where you are interviewed as a specialist by a podcast host	A "one sheet" that includes a short bio, downloadable photo, suggested title and questions for the host to ask you	1. OPN - hosts of top podcasts who target the same Audience as you	1. List building 2. Generating consults 3. Expanding your OPN network

A COUPLE OF IMPORTANT POINTS TO NOTE, WHICH APPLY TO THE CORPORATE AND CONSUMER MARKETS AS WELL...

I've excluded some of the traditionally recommended Audiences such as organic search/SEO, AdWords and other online advertising mediums such as Facebook.

That's not because they don't work as lead generators, but more because there are less expensive and/or faster methods that represent a wiser investment of your time and energy (and often at zero cost).

The above gives you a very valuable overview of the Leadsology LeadStreams® that can potentially work for you if you're serving the SME/solopreneur market.

Once again, however, in the interests of being direct and transparent, you need to be aware that each Leadsology LeadStream® can consist of a lot of moving parts.

As mentioned above, the main elements for each Leadsology LeadStream® are the Asset, the Audience, and the Persuasion Sequence.

To illustrate the point of there being many moving parts, here's a flow chart from an early iteration of our Boardroom Briefings.

CHART B

A special note for audio book listeners. in the book I present the chart which you'll find in a downloadable PDF. It's available to you as part of your purchase. I recommend that you pause the recording at this point, download the PDF of Chart B Part 6 and view the chart. Then restart the recording.

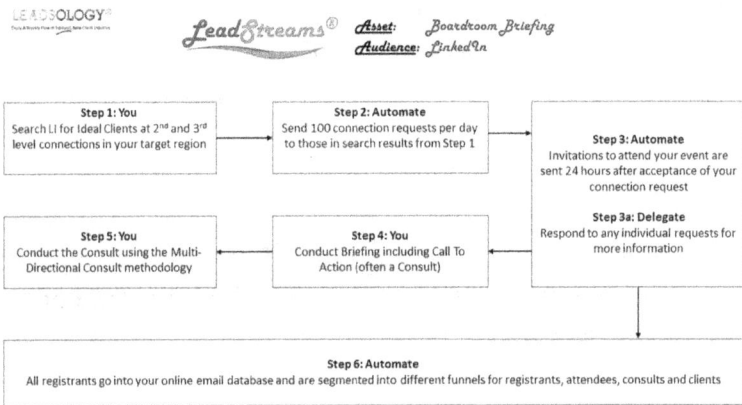

And here's a more detailed view in the form of a list of the Boardroom Briefings Sub-Elements:

A. Set up your LinkedIn profile (see image below)

B. Boolean LinkedIn search checklist

C. LinkedIn auto-connection and messaging platform

D. Online scheduling platform so people can register for the meeting

E. Online meeting platform

F. Online email database platform for storing registrant's details

G. API software to integrate the above three platforms

H. Reminder SMS and email system

I. PowerPoint presentation

J. Follow-up email sequence

Every sub-element has its own subtleties and nuances. Take the first item on the above list for example, which is how to set up your LinkedIn profile.

CHART C

A special note for audio book listeners. in the book I present the chart which you'll find in a downloadable PDF. It's available to you as part of your purchase. I recommend that you pause the recording at this point, download the PDF of Chart C Part 6 and view the chart. Then restart the recording.

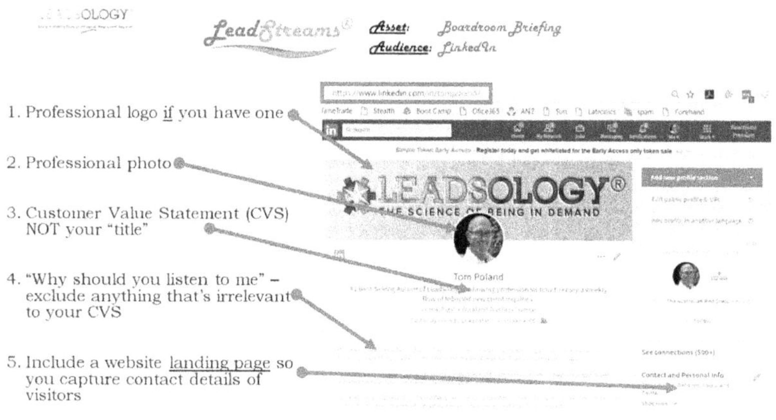

As you can see, setting up your LinkedIn profile alone is a combination of five different parts.

Some of these things might seem minor, but it's often the little things that get us. Not so much the big things.

If you have any doubt about that, just ask yourself how many times you been bitten by an elephant versus a mosquito.

The "devil is in the details" as they say.

I'm mentioning this, once again in the interests of full and open disclosure, because I don't want you racing off and thinking that you know everything there is to know about how to successfully embed, for example, Boardroom Briefings into your business.

It's like the difference between getting a book on how to play tennis and expecting to successfully take on some of the world's best players, versus getting the book *and* a coach and then practicing your butt off so that you are continually improving your results. The latter is what you need to do with your marketing.

And if you consider that the tennis analogy and taking on the world's best is a bit of a stretch, just remember that that's the equivalent of what you're intending to do in regard to your competitors: take on some of the world's best and beat them at their own game.

LEADSOLOGY LEADSTREAMS® FOR THE CORPORATE MARKET

If you've just jumped to this section and skipped the section above on the SME/solopreneur market, please go back and read that section because there are key points I make that apply to this section as well.

Here's some of the Leadsology LeadStreams® that are currently working well for the Corporate market.

CHART D

A special note for audio book listeners. in the book I present the chart which you'll find in a downloadable PDF. It's available to you as part of your purchase. I recommend that you pause the recording at this point, download the PDF of Chart D Part 6 and view the chart. Then restart the recording.

LeadStream®	Primary Asset	Best Audiences	Purpose
Published author Just like me but focused on your area of expertise, your Magic	The book	1. Amazon and in particular utilizing Amazon Marketing Services to target the right Audience 2. Your own email list 3. OPN email list 4. Any speaking opportunity	1. List building (always have something at the start of the book that drives readers to a landing page where they can opt in for a free resource) 2. Generating consults 3. Building your reputation as a credible, specialized expert
Lunch and Learns Offline gathering of executives from different companies who are interested in learning about how others are handling shared challenges.	PowerPoint presentation*	1. Your own email list 2. OPN email list 3. LinkedIn	1. Generating consults 2. List building
Diagnostic Online, in depth series of questions that automatically produces a customized report including recommendations.	Extensive online diagnostic platform	1. OPN email list 2. Your own list (once a year)	1. List-building 2. BBB

LeadStream®	Primary Asset	Best Audiences	Purpose
Survey Short series of questions that identify needs relevant to your service as well as offering a bench-marking report to respondents	An online survey platform and questions.	1. OPN lists 2. Your own list (once a year)	1. List building 2. Generating consults

It's worth noting also that there are quite a few variables that determine which Asset/Audience is the best combination, and that includes the size of your average sale and your average profit per sale, the lifetime value of your client (the total average transaction over the period that a client typically stays with you) and whether or not other lead generators are more efficient and/or more effective.

LEADSOLOGY LEADSTREAMS® FOR THE CONSUMER MARKET

Once again, if you skipped the above two sections on Leadsology LeadStreams® for the other two main markets please go back and read them because of made points in those two sections which are equally pertinent to the consumer market.

Here's a look at some of the Leadsology LeadStreams® are currently working well for the consumer market.

CHART E

A special note for audio book listeners. in the book I present the chart which you'll find in a downloadable PDF. It's available to you as part of your purchase. I recommend that you pause the recording at this point, download the PDF of Chart E Part 6 and view the chart. Then restart the recording.

LeadStream®	Primary Assets	Best Audiences	Purpose
Livestreams Typically, a training or discussion meeting with your WebCam on simulating a public speaking event	Whiteboard or flipchart presentation and WebCam together with quality microphone	1. Your own email list 2. OPN email list 3. Facebook	1. Building a Facebook Group membership 2. Generating sales 3. Keeping your brand in the brain of your network until they are ready to buy (BBB)
Five-day challenge A series of daily training and action challenges typically presented through short videos and designed to give participants a taste of the transformation you offer	Training videos and training page for each day	1. OPN email list 2. Your own list (once a year)	1. List-building 2. BBB
Internet Search Where you are interviewed as a specialist by a podcast host	Keyword research and matching landing page	1. SEO organic search results 2. AdWords paid search results	1. List building by driving people to a landing page on your website 2. Product sales and new client bookings

LeadStream®	Primary Assets	Best Audiences	Purpose
Boot Camp Five intense training webinars, presented one day after the other	Five Power-Point pre-sentations, sequence of launch emails, boot camp emails and follow-up emails	1. OPN email list 2. Your own list (once a year)	1. List-building 2. BBB

THE NATURE OF STREAMS AND LEADSOLOGY® LEADSTREAMS®

Leadsology LeadStreams® have a lot of characteristics in common with physical flows of water, be they streams or rivers.

We can learn a lot from nature and particularly in respect to these common characteristics.

For example, streams and rivers can:

1. Change direction

2. Suffer from a decrease in flow rate

3. Flood

4. Narrow

5. Widen

6. Go underground

7. Benefit thousands of people who have access to the stream

8. Dry up through overuse

9. Become polluted by thoughtful and uncaring users

That's just nine things that can happen to a river or stream and changes that Leadsology LeadStreams® are equally susceptible to.

What's the moral of the story here?

Simple: unlike commonly taught mythology, no lead generation stream is "set it and forget it."

You must continually trial, observe, and refine, and at every point measure the results of every part of your stream.

I mentioned at the start that Leadsology® is like a science and, that being the case, we need robust tracking and measuring systems in place so that we can reach conclusions which are both accurate and timely about which part of our Leadsology Lead-Stream® is functioning well and which parts need some refining to improve results.

For example, with our Boardroom Briefings, we measure the following parts of the stream:

1. Number of LinkedIn connection request made.

2. Number of LinkedIn connection requests accepted.

3. Number of LinkedIn boardroom briefing invitations resulting in registrations.

4. Number of registrants who attended.

5. Number of attendees who requested consult.

6. Number of consults that converted clients.

7. Average transaction value.

8. Cost per client acquisition.

Every single one of those items is a variable and many of them produce ratios, e.g. the ratio of registrants to attendees.

And every variable and every ratio is an opportunity to trial a variation, to fail or succeed, and thereby continually seek to improve the results of items #2 through to item #8.

In Part Six, I'll share with you how we make this tracking and measuring process both timely, accurate, and relatively simple and easy using our Marketing Dashboard.

MISTAKES AND THE SUPERFLUOUS

It can be quite helpful to have a look at some of the common traps that people fall into when attempting to embed the lead-generation systems into their businesses.

So, to save you some of the angst that others may have experienced, here is a handful of ideas that fall into the category of cautionary advice that will hopefully save you considerable angst.

TRAP NUMBER ONE: TEACHING YOURSELF MARKETING

I know that it's tempting, especially if someone feels that they have a limited budget, to try to teach themselves lead generation.

There is no question that you escape that category because you've quite wisely invested in this book and, therefore, you've demonstrated an awareness that self-learning alone is a long and torturous road, with multitudinous dead-end detours, far too many ups and downs, and innumerable potholes along the way.

TRAP NUMBER TWO: DO-IT-YOURSELF MARKETING

When I wanted to climb one of the world's most dangerous mountains, Mount Cook in New Zealand, it had the unenviable reputation of having killed more climbers than Mount Everest.

While Mount Cook is considerably smaller than Mount Everest, it's very prone to storms, avalanches, and hidden crevasses that add up to a cocktail of risk.

So, I hired a guide because, first, I wanted to reach the top of the mountain, but secondly, and far more importantly, I wanted to get safely back off the mountain.

Too many people before me had achieved the first objective, but sadly not the second one.

And marketing is like that.

There's a pretty good chance that you'll fall victim to some of the marketing storms, avalanches, and crevasses as you're trying to climb your marketing mountain.

So, do yourself a favor and find yourself a marketing guide. Someone who can walk with you every step of the way and show you the fastest and most secure way to the summit and back down again.

That guide certainly does not need to be me or one of my partners. You can find another guide who you can trust and who has been up and down the mountain successfully hundreds of times, but by all means hire them.

But by going it alone, you will at best waste years in trying to reach the summit and are far more likely to never make it that far.

TRAP NUMBER THREE: OFFERING ATTENDANCE BONUSES FOR EVENTS

As a professional, the success of quite a lot of your marketing and consults is dependent on people showing up.

It's therefore tempting to consider the use of a bonus to incentivize people to attend a webinar or a Boardroom Briefing-style meeting. Something like a bonus e-book or a mind map summarizing a certain message or strategy.

Here's my take on attendance bonuses.

If someone is not prepared to attend a meeting for the sake of the value they see in that meeting, then you're either trying to get the wrong person to the meeting, or you failed to clearly articulate the value in attending.

Either way, offering an attendance bonus won't help.

If you've got the right person and you've clearly articulated the value in attending, they will show up regardless of whether you are offering an attendance bonus or not.

Worse, if someone who is not a great prospect saw that you were offering an attendance bonus which was a prize draw for a trip to two to Paris, then yes, they'll show up, but for the wrong reason.

I learned this the hard way in 1997 when I ran a referral incentive competition and offered everyone who submitted referrals an entry into the prize draw for a trip for two to Fiji. Our ideal clients were small business owners.

We had a flood of referrals all right.

For example, we had the guy servicing the photocopier fill out a referral form with five of the names of his fellow photo copier-servicing colleagues. Not exactly our target market.

He wasn't filling out the referral form because these people needed our business training services; he was filling out the form because he wanted a free holiday in Fiji with his wife. And who can blame him?

The bottom line with attendance bonuses is that if you put the right value proposition in front of the right Audience, you don't need them, and the people who attend because of the bonus are not the people you want.

TRAP NUMBER FOUR: BEING CHEAP ON PRESENTATION GRAPHICS

It seems like a lot of people are tempted to put together Power-Point presentations or e-books using off-the-shelf software such as Microsoft Word or Microsoft PowerPoint or the equivalent Apple products.

If someone is in the bargain-basement market, and they are trying to be the cheapest guy or gal around and they want to attract clients who value cheap (good luck to them), then by all means they should produce a document or presentation that looks like their 12-year-old designed it for their school project.

But if you want to earn the right to attract top-quality clients and charge them premium prices, then you need to invest a few dollars in premium presentations.

And really, today the services of professional graphic designers through websites such as **www.upwork.com** are relatively inexpensive compared to yesteryear.

For example, I can have a 50-slide PowerPoint presentation made to look unbelievably professional and infinitely more engaging for around $450.

When you consider that I can use that one presentation perhaps 50 times a year over several years and generate literally thousands of new subscribers and hundreds of thousands in revenue, the $450 is a significantly worthwhile investment.

Similarly, I can have new logos created for $75 and e-books beautifully formatted for $175.

I certainly appreciate that, for some folk out there, spending even $75 is a bigger ask than it is for others.

So, do what you can with what you have. That's all that any of us can do.

But don't fool yourself about whether you can or cannot afford a thing.

Most of the people who say they can't afford a thing are really saying they prefer to spend their money on something else.

I'll be the first to admit that I get caught up in some "stingy-thinking" from time to time.

For example, I was considering experimenting with creating a new Leadsology LeadStream® and hiring someone for $550 to take some of the grunt work out of my life in the testing phase.

I decided that I would sit on that decision.

A few days later, I found myself considering upgrading my espresso machine for a cost of $800.

You should note that there is nothing wrong with my current espresso machine, but I just love a new gadget!

As I was salivating while reading the shiny, colorful web page featuring the new espresso machine, I realized that I was considering spending $800 on something that I had absolutely no need for, while at the same time trying to save $550 on something that could give me many thousands of dollars return on investment.

Shame on me!

I immediately hired that contractor for $550 and, while the relationship is in its early days yet, indications are promising.

(And before you email me, because some people will, yes, I went ahead and bought the espresso machine as well. It's true: we can have the best of both worlds.)

Don't do yourself the disservice of convincing yourself that you can't afford to invest in the development of your marketing capability.

The way I see it, with your future prosperity on the line, I can't see how you can afford *not* to invest.

And certainly, if you can find a few hundred dollars to make your marketing Assets more professional, then do it.

PART FOUR:

MAXIMIZING THE RESULTS OF YOUR LEAD GENERATION EFFORTS WITH FIVE MAGIFICATION MODELS

IF **HUMAN HISTORY** has taught us anything, it is that everything can be improved.

Whether it's the wheel that we have improved upon since 3500 BC, Alexander Graham Bell's telephone in 1876 (my oh my, that's come a long way), Johannes Gutenberg's printing press in 1439 (hello Kindle!), we human beings just can't seem to leave a thing alone. Certainly, I can't.

According to a *Washington Post* article, there are 50 Intuit words for "snow," including words that describe a snow-frozen landscape and snow that falls softly, versus snow that's good for driving a sled on.

I guess that when your very existence depends upon a thing, then the society you live in becomes very motivated to understand that things have subtleties and nuances.

And is the same with marketing.

There are so many subtleties and nuances to every aspect of marketing, and each one is like a number in the combination code that gets you into a safe. One wrong turn and it doesn't work.

And that's why I put together this part of the book.

Part Four takes you on a journey where I magnify those subtleties and nuances with the objective of helping you develop a deeper understanding of what it takes to successfully lead an ideal client from not knowing who you are, to becoming an irresistible and indispensable part of your business.

Let's get started.

The Four Levels of Psychological Allure

HOW TO CREATE A STRONG AND ALL-BUT-IRRESISTIBLE MAGNETISM BETWEEN YOUR AUDIENCE AND YOURSELF

ALLURE CAN BE defined as the quality of being powerfully and mysteriously attractive or fascinating.

Fortunately for me, I'm not referring to physical allure, but more commercial allure.

Most marketers talk about the need to establish rapport with the prospect prior to asking for the sale.

And while that's very important and, indeed, a solid start, we can and should go well beyond having someone simply know and like us prior to suggesting that they might like to work with us.

By way of illustration, I mentioned earlier in this book that, when I first saw the woman who is now my wife, I fell in love at first sight.

I could have established rapport with her in the form of introducing myself and having her laugh at a couple of my jokes but that wouldn't have been nearly enough for me to meet with success in response to a proposal for marriage.

Most of my clients are asking their Audiences to part with a significant amount of money in return for the potential of gaining a return on that investment, be that a financial return or otherwise, that is greater than the investment that was asked for.

Given that to be the case, we need to do a heck of a lot more than just introducing ourselves to our Audiences and having them laugh at a couple of jokes.

That might get you success as a comedian doing stand-up, but it sure as heck isn't enough to have a senior executive authorize the transfer of $100,000 to your bank account, or for a business owner to commit $5,000 a month for your coaching services, or for a homeowner to agree that they'll invest $30,000 on your architectural services.

So, let's have a look at what it takes to create a situation where people are so powerfully attracted to the idea of working with you that they are literally tossing and turning in their bed the night before they are due to meet with you, worried about whether you'll accept them as a client.

I covered some of this subject in the section in Part Two about creating a marketing message and cascading that out into proprietary trademarks and unique value-delivery models. That's a pretty good place to start.

I've also said that identifying potential prospects is pretty much the easiest thing in the world to do. The tough part is taking them from having never heard of you to having them see you as the only option for solving their problem, overcoming their challenge, or fulfilling the potential of an opportunity.

And so, without further review, here are the four levels of creating Psychological Allure.

LEVEL 1: RAPPORT

The Cambridge English dictionary defines rapport as meaning having a good understanding of someone and able to communicate well with them.

Establishing a relationship with your Audience whereby they like you is enough to qualify for rapport in my book. Literally.

What helps to establish rapport is you being as relaxed, as genuine and as authentic, as true to your values, vision and personality, as you possibly can be.

The thing that will destroy rapport quickly is you trying to be the person that you think the Audience wants you to be.

Be conversational not only in your speaking but also in your writing. Be relaxed in your presentations.

I'm not saying this is always easy, but being relaxed is like anything else, the more you practice it the better you get at it.

One of the more pertinent observations offered by Neuro Linguistic Programming, or NLP as it become known, is that individuals and Audiences tend to mirror your behavior.

If they perceive that you're uptight, they become uptight.

It's probably some sort of prehistoric defense pattern that's designed to alert us to threats, but whatever the origin of this pattern, it's a reality today.

Likewise, if they perceive that you are relaxed, they relax. If they see you that you're smiling and having good time, they reciprocate.

When my clients are going to create a marketing Asset, such as an e-book or a book or a guide, I ask them to write it as if they were speaking to a good friend over coffee.

I do know that something can happen in some people's brains the moment they start to type. They go from thinking informally to thinking formally. This difference may have its origins in when we were at school, playing in the playground, versus writing in the classroom.

Again though, the reason we get screwed up like this is not as important as un-screwing ourselves and being the person we are, versus the person we think is going to be most acceptable to the Audience.

These days semi-miraculous software such as Nuance's "Dragon NaturallySpeaking," which I'm using to create this book, make it easier than ever to write in a manner which is closer to how we would talk.

That's because I'm not actually writing a book anymore; I'm speaking a book.

So, when you next want to produce an e-book or a special report or a guide of some sort, simply open a Word-style document, type up the outline, insert bullet points under each main section heading, refine it and then quit writing and start speaking to actually create the document.

That will help you to "write" in a way that is more relaxed, more authentic, and infinitely easier to read than a more formal treatment of the same subject.

As a bonus beyond the fact that you'll be able to produce a more readable, engaging, interesting, and rapport-building document, you also be able to do it in about half the time it would take you to type it, even assuming that you are an intermediate typist.

As for speaking and presenting in a more-relaxed manner, using the traditionally recommended technique of imagining someone in the Audience naked never worked for me. I found it more distracting than anything else; focusing on the most attractive member of the Audience and mentally undressing them was definitely not helping me to focus on delivery!

If you're going to be speaking to an Audience, whether it's to a physical Audience or a webinar, here's a recipe for relaxation.

The very first time you have to present, contrary to what most people recommend, I'd encourage you to write the whole darn thing out, word for word.

Then read that presentation to an imaginary Audience all the way through, 21 times.

Each time you read it, try to remember what's coming up next.

Once you've done that 21 times, you will have come pretty close to memorizing the whole thing, and that's the point where you reduce it to a series of chapter headings and bullet points.

Then you go through it again another seven times in rehearsal mode.

If you know exactly what you're going to say and how you can say it, then your stomach is going to feel less like it's got jumbo jets flying around in it and more like this just a few quiet butterflies gently flapping their wings.

In other words, it won't completely remove your nerves, but it'll certainly settle you down a lot.

The last thing to do is to sit down quietly prior to your presentation.

If this is a physical presentation were talking about, you'll be sitting in a seat waiting to be introduced. If it's a webinar or an online presentation, then you can simply sit in front of your computer.

Either way, you shut your eyes and you visualize a beach with a wave gently rolling in as you take a long, slow, relaxed inhale. Then you do the same for the exhale, only visualizing the wave slowly retreating down the beach. As you visualize the waves coming in, you quietly say to yourself, "I'm feeling calm," and as the wave goes out you tell yourself, "I'm feeling relaxed."

The mind and the body have a most marvelous interconnection in that they both listen to each other.

Get your mind to relax through breathing gently and fully and your body will relax, and as your body relaxes, your mind follows suit and the cycle of relaxation progresses.

Left to its own devices, your mind will pick up tension from your body and your body will pick up tension from your mind, and you'll end up in a vicious cycle of tension and anxiety.

Think of the above structure as being like scaffolds around a new building. Very necessary to secure safe and rapid growth as the building goes up, but once the building is complete, you can take the scaffolding down.

And as you build your speaking capability you can slowly move away from the recommended structure above because you simply won't need it.

If I was attending a workshop and the organizer rushed up to me and told me that the speaker they had lined up for that day was ill and asked me if I could take their place and that I'd have to start in five minutes, I'd be totally cool with that and wouldn't need to go through the process that I've described above.

But before my first fully-fledged public speaking gig, I did exactly what I recommended above that you do.

In summary, the more relaxed you are, the more relaxed your Audience will be, and the faster you'll be able to establish rapport by communicating effectively with them.

Level 2: Respect

You gain respect when a person admires your abilities, qualities, and achievements.

You can begin to build respect through your bio and continue to build it by fulfilling Woody Allen's admonition that "80 percent of success in life is showing up"), and therefore go one better and show up on time, start meetings on time, and finish them on time.

The interesting thing about respect is that it is context-specific.

What I mean by that is that people will generally only value the respect you may have built, if it's relevant to their needs, values, or wants.

For example, if I've completed an Ironman triathlon, or raced in the National Superbike competition, or climbed a mountain that's killed more people than Mount Everest, I may gain respect among people who are seeking a personal development coach.

But you won't hear any of those things mentioned if I'm speaking at a marketing conference, because they have no direct relevance for effective marketing.

What you may hear, however, is that prior to the Internet I was physically published in 27 countries, shared international speaking platforms with the likes of Michael Gerber of E-Myth fame and so on, and so on.

That's because I want to build respect in a context that's relevant to my Audience. Cut everything out of your bio that's not relevant to your subject and Audience.

And one of the simplest and easiest ways that you can build respect amongst your Audience is to demonstrate that you do what you tell people you're going to do.

For example, if you set the agenda for a meeting promising to disclose how to enjoy a five-fold increase in the flow of leads from any marketing campaign, you had better be very explicit and demonstrate exactly how to do that so you deliver on that promise (see The SEW Segmentation Formula that follows).

On that note, you'll also gain respect when you demonstrate the depth of your knowledge and capabilities.

I had a client call yesterday who wanted to invite his list to complete a short survey and then offer them a consult to see if what he offered was a fit for the needs of the respondents.

The problem is that, while a survey can be very effective at uncovering needs, it doesn't give him enough "real estate" in the form of time to establish respect for what he does.

To give him the real estate that will allow him to establish not just Rapport and Respect, but also the elements of Relatability and Reciprocity that I'll discuss in a moment, I recommended that he offer a training webinar to address the needs identified in the survey, in between the survey and the consult.

There's a very high likelihood that you are marketing to a relatively sophisticated Audience, as opposed to say an Audience of 18-year-olds who are hoping to get rich quick before the age of 21, and who are therefore more inclined to believe the BS and hype promoted by the get-rich-quick charlatans.

But if I'm right about your Audience, they have been bitten before and now possess highly sensitive BS radars. They may be open-minded (most people who attend a training session or buy a book possess that characteristic) and want to learn, but they are also going to be skeptical.

And that's why I do my darndest to never give anyone even a whiff of hype.

It's pretty rare that I slip up and say something like "everyone" and "no one" unless it's literally true. For example, somewhere above you'll see these words:

Frankly, getting new clients on board is the reason why virtually everyone in a professional services business writes a book.

Note the word "virtually."

It may seem pedantic, but by my estimate, 20 percent of your Audience will decide that you're either the real deal or you're a hype-merchant like "the rest of them," based on whether you are being accurate with your statements.

Once again, we find that the devil is in the details.

Level 3: Relatability

Another fundamental truth of humans is that we seek out relationships.

And that's why I encourage my clients to write in a conversational style, because it's easier for the reader to relate to my client as a real human being when reading something that's written as if they were personally being addressed.

Allow me to illustrate my point by describing a conversation I had with a client yesterday.

You may recall that when I write a book I set aside 7 to 9 days and go flat out and "download."

Yesterday was such a day.

But I had also scheduled a client meeting with Thomas, a merger and acquisition consultant and trainer living in Bonn, Germany.

We had a little chit chat at the start of our meeting and he asked what I've been up to during the day, given that the time of the meeting was at the start of his day and at the end of mine.

I explained to him that I'd been writing this book and I also explained that it wasn't really writing, since I use dictation software, so that really, I was speaking this book.

Now, while it's true that most people suddenly become more formal when they write as compared to when they speak, this is true in the extreme for Germans.

Not only do Germans have both formal and informal versions of their spoken language, depending on how well they know a person, their writing style in any business context is formal in the extreme.

You needed to know that to understand Thomas' next comment which was something to the effect of, "wow, I'm really impressed that you can speak in a way that people write."

"No no no", I replied, "what's impressive is the person who can write in a way that people speak."

By way of further validation, have a look at the advertisements on television and notice how many of them show happy, relaxed, casual, smiling, friendly people demonstrating/promoting/engaging with the product or service on offer.

The largest soft drink company in the world and the largest fast-food franchise chain in the world don't have someone in their advertisements sitting at a desk reading a statement that sounds like the latest earnings report from a bank.

Likewise, if you want to increase Relatability with your Audience, relax and speak/write as if you were addressing one person, personally.

And to that end, always sprinkle the words "you" and "your" liberally throughout your text or conversation to have each reader or listener feel like that you're addressing them personally and directly.

I'll talk about how to increase Relatability more later in this section when we deal with the Leadsology® Persuasion Sequence.

Level 4: Reciprocity

In the 1960s, a new field of psychology was developing, called Transactional Analysis, and in the first half of that decade psychologist Eric Berne wrote a seminal work on the subject entitled *The Games People Play*.

In what was a relatively short book, Berne simply and clearly articulated the fact that human beings like to "keep the score even," as I refer to it.

If I'm walking down the road and someone walking toward me says "Hi Tom!" then according to Berne, he/she has given me two credits, one for saying hello and the other for saying my name.

If I've forgotten that person's name and weakly respond with a simple "hello" then I feel stink because they gave me two credits and I only responded with one.

Similarly, if I pick up a call and it's a friend inviting us to dinner, naturally I ask what we can bring.

Later, when I tell my wife about the invitation, she'll ask me what our friends suggested we bring to the dinner.

Invariably, I'll repeat what our friend suggested, which was "you don't need to bring anything, please don't bring anything, definitely don't bring anything."

My wife of course will have to bring something. A bottle of wine, some flowers, a small gift… anything that will be perceived as commensurate value in exchange for the dinner invitation.

She must be careful not to overdo it though, because if she gives the bottle of wine <u>and </u>the bunch of flowers<u> and</u> the small gift, then you can bet your bottom dollar that the morning after the dinner there's a gift from our hosts on the front doorstep, and so the dance of reciprocity continues.

What does this all mean to you as a marketer?

Simple: if you will give your Audience what they want (remember: honey pots outside the forest to attract the bears) in the form of free Assets which are valuable and interesting, then their subconscious psychological inclination, if not compulsion, will be to work with you in preference to your competitors.

Almost the only exception to this will be the member of an Audience who chooses to work with someone else, when they could have chosen you, because that someone else is a very close relative. It's rare that you'll be able to trump blood with brains.

How to Increase Your Flow of Leads Five-Fold

Use My SEW Audience Segmentation Formula

I'VE WRITTEN A lot about your Audience, but I'm in danger of at best being inaccurate, or at worst being misleading, without diving deeper into the subject and making some distinctions about your Audience, in much the same way that the Intuit makes distinctions about snow.

The fact is that you don't have an Audience.

You have at the very least, three Audiences.

I discovered this some years ago when I set up a new website, and in conjunction with launching a book, I created a lot of opportunities for people who purchased the book, to go from the book to my website and subscribe in exchange for me giving them a honey pot.

My goal in doing so was to convert people from being purchasers of my book into being subscribers. When you sell a book on Amazon you have no idea who bought that book, but by putting some honey pots outside of the book forest, you'll be able to tempt some of the bears to come on out.

(And if you have no idea what I was just writing about then you need to reread the Preface!)

This was the first time I'd gone to the time and trouble of creating multiple landing pages offering free honey pots and promoting them through the sale of the book.

This, combined with information from our online email platform, which stores the contact details of those who opt in via one of our landing pages, provided me with the insights that resulted in the identification of these three Audience segments.

In other words, for the first time, I was able to track the honey pot behavior of each individual from the time they opted in through to the time they purchased.

And that's what led to my discovery that, in fact, we have at least three Audiences and that we would be wise to cater to each of them.

I call these Audiences the Seekers, the Explorers, and the Wanderers, hence the term SEW Segmentation Formula.

Let's have a closer look at each segment so I can explain how you can generate maximum results by catering to each of their needs.

THE SEEKERS

By tracking the behavior of people who opted into one of our landing pages, I was able to accurately conclude that 3 percent of my Audiences invested in my services almost immediately after engaging one of my honey pots/Assets.

This manifested in someone who bought my book, went from my book to my website, downloaded a free something in exchange for the contact details and was back the same day or the next day investing in my program.

(Right now, you can't join my program online, you have to go to **www.BookAChatWithTom.com** and book a time for us to talk so we can figure out which of the various options to work with me would be the best fit for your needs.)

Likewise, 3 percent of people attending a webinar or listening to me being interviewed on a podcast or hearing me speak at a conference decided pretty much straight away that I had what they were looking for.

The primary characteristic of the Seekers is that they are actively seeking a solution for the problem/challenge/opportunity and that's why I call them the Seekers.

Their second characteristic is that they are fast decision-makers. They don't mess around. They know what they want and when they see it, they buy, and they buy fast.

In addition, Seekers have moved beyond a need to validate you or your brand and they simply need to confirm that whatever it is you're offering is a fit for their needs. And that's why you should offer them either an opportunity to buy immediately by creating a sales page on your website, or giving them a landing page where they can immediately book time to talk with you.

If you have not developed any such honey pots, that is pretty likely the only way you're going to get new business from word-of-mouth referrals.

Outside of that, if you want to help the Seekers part with the money that's burning a hole in their pocket, you need to create some honey pots in the form of Educational Marketing Assets (EMA), such as books, E-guides, or webinars, because Seekers are serious about digging deep and those type of Assets help them do that.

(Don't get confused by me referring to an Asset as an Educational Marketing Asset or EMA; they are one in the same thing. But the latter term more fully describes the nature of the honey pots/ Assets within a marketing context).

THE EXPLORERS

As mentioned, by tracking the opt-in behavior of visitors to our website, we were able to determine that 3 percent of people who engaged with my brand via one of our Assets chose to invest almost immediately after that engagement.

But I noticed a larger group within my Audience who needed multiple honey pot experiences of my brand before they bought.

I call this segment the Explorers because they have a need to explore what I have to offer, across multiple experiences, or EMAs as I referred to above.

For example, an Explorer may download my interactive Leadsology® Model, and five minutes later they're back completing my lead-generation Diagnostic tool and the next week they are attending a webinar training, completing my Survey, and finally booking a time to talk with me.

Explorers typically need five exposures to your brand in the form of EMAs before they'll buy, and they make up 12 percent of an Audience. And so, when you successfully cater to them, you'll grow the number of new client inquiries five times over, because you've now gone from catering to only 3 percent of your Audience, to a total of 15 percent.

(Don't get hung on the numbers here. As mentioned, Explorers make up 12 percent of my Audience and, while the percentage of people making up each of these three segments in your Audiences may vary, the principle remains the same in that you need to cater to all three segments. Otherwise, you're leaving a lot of money on the table.)

Explorers share the same primary characteristic as the Seekers, in that they are actively looking for a solution to their problem/challenge/opportunity.

But the difference between the two segments is that the Explorer's other primary characteristic is that they are by nature more cautious buyers.

Putting this another way, if a Seeker is 100 percent committed to buying right now, an Explorer is also 100 percent committed to buying, but not right now.

The Explorers want to take time to validate not only your integrity and your ability to deliver on your promise, but they also need to validate, endlessly it would seem, the fit between their needs and your solution.

The third point of validation the Explorer seeks has nothing to do with you or your service, but rather with their ability to implement your recommendations and thereby benefit from them. More on that soon.

As mentioned above, the Seekers are relatively easy to cater to. You just give them a call to action (CTA) in the form of a buying link, or a link to book a time to talk with you.

But if that's all you provide, then you're going to be leaving a lot of money on the table, because there are four times as many Explorers as there are Seekers.

The moral of the story with Explorers is that you need to be able to offer them multiple EMAs to satisfy their need for exploration.

If you fail to provide them with that opportunity, then you fail to satisfy their need and they'll go someplace else to have that need met: i.e., your competitors.

Catering to the Explorers is simple: develop multiple honey pots and offer them for free on your website. If you want to see examples, then naturally you can go to my website at **www.leadsology.guru** for "swipe and deploy" inspiration.

Some of my most effective Explorer assets allow this Audience segment to dive deep and thoroughly investigate my brand and they include:

- ✓ My five-day lead-generation challenge at **www.leadsology.guru/five-day-challenge**
- ✓ My lead-generation diagnostic tool at **www.leadsology.guru/diagnostic**
- ✓ And my five-day lead generation Boot Camp, which I run once a year, and various training webinars.

Having said that catering to the Explorers is simple, I'll be the first to admit that it's not easy.

Developing multiple EMAs takes time, imagination, and a deeper level of understanding of exactly which Assets to put in front of your Audience.

But don't do what I did and develop five EMAs almost simultaneously. Instead, preserve your sanity and your marriage by developing them one at a time.

If you create a landing page that offers an EMA targeting Explorers, then you need to bear in mind that this segment is looking for a depth of information that the Wanderers don't need or want.

To that extent, a landing page for an Explorer would ideally include a short video that gives them details about both the features and benefits of what you're offering to them.

By contrast, as you'll discover in a moment, landing pages for the Wanderers should contain little more than a headline featuring the benefit of your offer and a click CTA, without videos or paragraphs and pages of text.

THE WANDERERS

According to the results of our tracking and measuring, 85 percent of our Audience has no serious intent to buy. Rather, they're content to wander through your EMA like they are strolling down a garden path and pausing to smell the roses without any intent to buy a bunch.

It would be easy to dismiss the Wanderers as being a waste of your time.

But nothing could be further from the truth.

Firstly, a small number of the Wanderers have it in their DNA to be advocates for the things they like the look of.

Some of these people will never buy from you, but they may read your book or come to your boardroom briefing and, when they are having coffee with a friend who clearly has a need for what you have to offer, their referral will be made and then you'll be very happy that you welcomed the Wanderers along with the other segments.

The second reason why the Wanderers are far from a waste of time is that there is a significant percentage of them that, over time, you may be able to shift from having no awareness of their need for what you offer to having a moderate awareness, and finally to a heightened awareness.

In other words, with the right EMA sequence, you can transform a Wanderer into an Explorer and then into a Seeker.

You gain the attention of a Wanderers by invoking curiosity, and their primary need is to be tempted with the promise of entertainment and/or education.

The type of EMA that works well for Wanderers is something that ticks each of the "Short, Simple, and Shiny" boxes.

If you go to my website, you'll be able to download the full interactive, one-page Leadsology® Model, and that's a perfect example of something that's Short, Simple, and Shiny.

A "one-page something" that offers valuable information in the form of a model or a blueprint or a checklist or a flowchart or a template or a cheat sheet... is exactly what you need to entice both the Explorers and the Wanderers into swapping the contact details on the landing page for your one-page honey pot.

You'll recall my admonition to have something that sustains BBB (your brand in their brain until they are ready to buy) and this is especially important for the Wanderers.

Autoresponders (Google it), blog posts, tweets, podcasts, regular webinars, a quote of the week, Facebook group posts, and LinkedIn are just some of the ways that you may choose to include in your marketing mix, so you can successfully BBB and thereby be top-of-mind when the Wanderer is suddenly feeling in the mood to become a Seeker.

In conclusion, you can increase the number of leads you generate more than fivefold by catering to the needs of all three segments in your Audiences.

HOW TO SHIFT WANDERERS TO EXPLORERS

Imagine that you're out on a nice Sunday morning walk in the woods or forest.

You start out on your little hike intending just to stroll through the natural beauty surrounding you and to breathe in the fresh air.

But a short way into your walk, something sparkling attracts your attention.

You stop and look in the direction of the sparkling object and you see that the sun is bouncing of what looks a piece of glass.

Being the environmentally-caring person you are, you walk some 20 meters off the track, through some trees, intending to pick up the glass and deposit it later in recycle bin.

But as you approach the source of the sparkle, you see that it's not a fragment of glass but rather a large diamond.

You can't believe your good luck.

You pick up the diamond, examine it closely and slide it securely into a zipped pocket somewhere on your clothes.

Now, if that happened, what would be the very next thing you would do?

I mean, the very next thing.

As in immediately, even before you took another step.

You'd look around to see if there were any more diamonds, right?

You betcha.

And suddenly, you've gone from being a Wanderer, to an Explorer.

And that shows you how to shift your Wandering Audience to your Exploring Audience — by wowing them with unexpected value.

And that brings us nicely to the fourth of our five Magnification Models which is…

The Titanium Triangle: Creating an Inexhaustible Flow of Leads

I **CHOSE THE WORD** "Titanium" to represent the idea of being indestructible, together with being valuable.

Titanium has what referred to as the "highest specific strength" of all metals, is totally resistant to corrosion, is very lightweight and, thus, is more valuable than gold.

And of course, we all know that a triangle has three sides.

So, when we put the two ideas together in the phrase "Titanium Triangle," and we employ that phrase in the context of lead generation, it adequately describes a model which has three sides to it and is both indestructible and highly valuable.

More specifically, the Titanium Triangle offers a "big picture" of how to create a continual supply of high-quality new client inquiries flowing into your business virtually every single week of the year.

Side #1: List Building

Side #1 requires you to do something, virtually every single week of the year, to build your list of email subscribers.

For example, most weeks of the year, someone else is promoting me to their list, either because I've been interviewed by them, or because they liked the idea of offering one of my honey pots (e.g., my **five-day lead generation challenge**) because they feel their Audience will benefit.

Also, most days of the year, I have a book or two being promoted on Amazon and am, therefore, in the face of prospective new Audience members who purchase a book, which then leads them to one of my free offers (read "EMA" or "honey pot") on my website, for which they provide their contact details.

Side # 2: Call To Action (CTA)

Side #2 requires you do something, virtually every single week of the year, that asks members of your Audience to act.

For example, at least 30 times a year, I present the webinar to an OPN Audience.

It's worthwhile noting that, while webinars are not as good as they used to be for generating clients directly or even for generating consults, they are still right up there as one of the best list-builders of all time, because every single registrant is legitimately added to your email list.

At the end of that webinar, I invite attendees to visit my landing page where they can read about how they might qualify to book a time to speak with me about their lead-generation needs and learn whether I have something that might fit those needs.

An effective CTA almost without exception consists of one single option that you give an Audience to accept or decline.

For example, that means when it comes time for your CTA, you don't offer a consult, urge them to buy a downloadable course, and also offer them another free honey pot.

But while your CTA normally offers only one action, it may offer alternative ways to take that action, such as clicking on an online booking scheduling link, sending an SMS to your mobile phone, or emailing you, and so on.

The result of your CTA is the most important number that you need to track and measure. For example, the number of people who have booked a time to talk with me about potentially becoming a client, or what I would call a consult, is the most important number that I track (see "Your number one number" in Part One.

Almost all professionals should use consult-type meetings as the primary number to track and measure with the objective of predicting the future health of their business.

New leads, flowing into your business, are, in effect, the lifeblood of your business. As such, they warrant careful attention in the form of attracting and measuring.

A CAUTIONARY NOTE ON CTAs

Vic was a new Presbyterian minister when he gave his very first sermon to his very first congregation.

It was, he said, full of fire and brimstone and promises of eternal damnation for those who refuse to repent their sins.

Feeling rather pleased with himself, after the service he positioned himself at the exit door to shake the hands of all the parishioners.

The very last parishioner to walk out of the church was a craggy-looking old Scotsman, complete with Tweed cap, a weather-beaten wrinkled face, and walking stick.

The old man took Vic's outstretched hand and clenched it with both of his hands in a grip that made Vic feel that his hand was being squeezed in a steel vice.

He then looked Vic right in the eye, so that he felt like his soul was being pierced.

At which point, Vic inquired somewhat weakly as to how he had enjoyed the sermon.

"Laddie," the old Scotsman commanded, "if you canna feed the sheep, dinna shear them."

You earn the right to shear the sheep.

You earn the right to deliver a CTA.

Of the thousands of people that I've delivered a CTA to, I'm not aware of even one objection or a complaint.

That's because I've built up such a high level of Rapport, Respect, Relatability and Reciprocity (remember them?), and secondly because I don't engage in feverish pitches that stack layer upon layer of ridiculous and unbelievable offers combined with bonus offers of Ginsu steak knives, or whatever.

As mentioned above, I invariably embed a CTA at the end of my webinar presentations, but I also sprinkle them judiciously throughout my five-day lead generation challenge, and at the end of pretty much every other honey pot/EMA, such as a diagnostic tool, an e-guide, book, survey, and so on.

Feed the sheep first, then offer to shear them. That way you keep all your marketing in the win-win zone.

Side # 3: BBB

Side #3 requires you to do something, virtually every single week of the year, that keeps your Brand in your Audience's Brain until they are ready to Buy.

A BBB Asset is the same as an EMA, in that it needs to be matched to the market.

For example, many busy executives and entrepreneurs love podcasts because they allow them to learn while they fly, drive, and exercise, whereas blogs won't be consumed at the same rate unless your name is Seth Godin, arguably the most popular business blogger in the world, who is smart enough to limit his blogs to around a 22-second read.

Horses for courses.

Personally, I use a VLOGcast for my BBB Asset.

The term VLOG has its origins in blogs and simply means that you're producing a video blog instead of a written one. That can mean that you stare at the camera and talk instead of writing, or it can mean that you interview someone with WebCams on, which is what I do.

After the interview is finished, it gets produced and we strip off the audio and publish it as a podcast and we have a transcript created of the audio so that we can also offer a downloadable PDF.

I thought that I'd invented the term VLOGcast, but when I do a Google search for it, I find over 51,000 hits. Apparently, at least one other person out of the 7.6 billion people on the planet had the same good idea at the same time.

The reason that I re-purposed the original video interview into a podcast and transcript is simply because I want to be able to cater to as many of my Audience's media preferences as possible.

I use a "7 questions in 7 minutes" format and so, by the time I've greeted my guest, tested his/her audio, then introduced them, conducted the interview, and wrapped up, I've got the whole thing done in under 30 minutes, including editing and uploading. My assistant then can strip off the audio for the podcast, have it transcribed for the PDF download, and publish it to the various platforms that we use.

And even better, I don't chase anyone for interviews, because I have contractors find the people who would make for great interviewees, and the latter book their session using my online scheduling link.

The other reason for re-purposing the VLOG into a podcast and transcript is that, really, we've done all the heavy lifting when we identified the guest, approached them and got them to book for the session, and conducted/recorded it.

It takes very little extra work to then re-purpose the same content across different mediums and thereby maximize our Audience's uptake.

CONCLUSION

Your objective is to have virtually every single week of the year filled with something that builds your list, puts a CTA in front of your Audience, and keeps your brand in their brain until ready to buy.

And don't get hung up on having all three operating from next week.

The power is in beginning.

I'd recommend you start with one list-builder, once a month, work your way up to once a week, and then start adding your CTAs and BBBs.

The Leadsology®
Persuasion Sequence

A Ten-Step Sequence That Motivates an Audience to Want to Know More

Introduction

Imagine a 100-meter running track and that a prospect is standing at the start line and he/she sees a pot of gold at the finish line.

In this analogy, the pot of gold represents the value proposition that's embedded in your marketing message: e.g., "Enjoy a weekly flow of inbound new client inquiries."

That's the picture: your prospect standing at that start line eyeing the pot of gold at the finish link, 100 meters away.

But your prospect is not moving and you wonder why.

After all, it's only 100 meters to the gold, so why are they still stuck on the starting line.

The answer is that they see something you don't, which is a series of hurdles between them and the pot of gold.

And the hurdles have names, like "Risk" and "Pricing" and "Features" and even more.

Now you can see what the prospect sees, that there are obstacles between him/her and the pot of gold that you're offering them.

And what effective marketing does is make those obstacles disappear from the mind of your prospect, one by one.

And that's what the Leadsology® Persuasion Sequence does too.

But there's more.

If you look back at the 100-meter track, you'll notice that, in addition to the hurdles, there are three alternate exits that could potentially divert your prospects journey away from your pot of gold to other pots of gold.

Those three detours have the street signs of "Direct Competitors," "Indirect Competitors," and "DIY" (or for Corporate clients "Do It In-house").

Effective marketing not only removes all of the hurdles from a prospect's mind, it also seals off all possible exits that might divert their attention from our pot of gold.

After all, the pot of gold at the end of our competitor's tracks are probably full of fool's gold and it's therefore in our prospect's best interest to not waste their time going down those detours.

And the Leadsology® Persuasion Sequence will reveal exactly how to remove the hurdles and seal off the exits.

But before we begin, let me remind you of the concept of Honey Pot marketing, a.k.a., Educational Marketing Asset (EMA), which is anything that educates a prospect by giving them valuable insights and implementable ideas in your areas of expertise.

Most people assume that the word "educational" is about upskilling the Audience with valuable ideas from your area of expertise, but it's also about educating them about why you are their #1 supplier of choice, and educating them as to why acting on your CTA (see above) is a wise decision.

In many cases, EMAs will motivate the right prospects to contact you to find out more about how you work with clients and to see if they can become one.

EMAs include webinars, seminars, workshops, books, challenges, and special reports (which I refer to as "guides"), and they are the subject of this document.

Other EMAs include diagnostic reports, surveys, and profiling tools, but I'm not going to address those here.

Instead, I'm going to focus on those EMAs that provide you with the real estate/time to build Rapport, Respect, Relatability and Reciprocity.

THE TEN STEPS I COVER IN THIS SEGMENT INCLUDE:

STEP ONE: Creating a compelling title.

STEP TWO: Embedding gold in your agenda.

STEP THREE: Establishing yourself as a wizard.

STEP FOUR: Offering the promise.

STEP FIVE: Describing the problem and symptoms of not having your service.

STEP SIX: Telling them what they have tried and why it didn't work.

STEP SEVEN: Revealing your model or a part thereof.

STEP EIGHT: Explaining why they should not attempt to implement on their own.

STEP NINE: Making your offer.

STEP TEN: A special note for books, special reports, and meetings.

Let's walk our way through each of the 10, step-by-step.

STEP ONE: CREATE A COMPELLING TITLE

PURPOSE

- Motivates your Audience to engage with your EMA.

OVERVIEW

- Audiences need a reason to invest time and energy in your EMA and a benefit-rich title has that reason embedded in it.

WHY THIS IS IMPORTANT

- You are competing against myriad other options that your Audience have available to choose from, so you need a value proposition in your title that cuts through those other options and compels a person to engage.

HOW THIS CAN BE ACHIEVED

- Use your marketing message (see Part Two of Leadsology®: Marketing The Invisible) or a variation of that: e.g., *"How to create a flow of high quality, inbound, new client inquires virtually every week of the year"* or *"How to increase productivity by 25 percent or more in just eight weeks"*

- The above titles stimulate desire-based motivation and, to add even more power, you can use a subtitle that simulates legitimate fear-based motivation in the form of mistakes to avoid: e.g., *"Plus seven common but costly marketing mistakes to avoid."*

- Note that if you are promoting your title via the internet (e.g. webinars), you need a short title so that it's mobile phone-friendly.

STEP TWO: EMBED GOLD IN YOUR AGENDA/TABLE OF CONTENTS

PURPOSE

- Further motivates your Audience to engage with your EMA.

- Reinforces the perception of differentiation.

OVERVIEW

- Content can be made up of different segments and each segment can be given a special name or title: e.g., "The Four Levels of Psychological Allure," or "The Titanium Triangle," which arouses curiosity and hints that you have something proprietary and valuable to share.

WHY THIS IS IMPORTANT

- While an effective title motivates people to find out more about your EMA, Embedded Gold in your agenda or table of contents motivates them to buy the book or download the guide or register for the meeting.

HOW THIS CAN BE ACHIEVED

- Try not to fall into the trap of thinking that you need a logical flow throughout your EMA. Instead, think of your EMA content as consisting of a series of valuable segments without the need to "bridge" from one to the next, which is what you need to do if you were writing a novel.

- Follow the steps and structure outlined in this segment but use proprietary titles (see above examples) to introduce your segments within each part of your EMA, most especially for steps Five, Six and Seven.

- Use your imagination and ask, "what's this like?" to stimulate your mind into creative mode: e.g., a product or service that people love or hate can be labeled a "Black Jellybean."

STEP THREE: ESTABLISH YOURSELF AS A WIZARD

PURPOSE

- Opens the mind.

OVERVIEW

- A Wizard has Magic in the form of the power to transform the Audience's problems into solutions, pain into pleasure, dissatisfaction into fulfillment, and effort into flow.

- The idea is to position yourself as someone prospects think they need more than you need them. This reverses the normal psychology of selling, which is where the prospect perceives that the supplier wants to make a sale more than they want to buy.

WHY THIS IS IMPORTANT

- So that your Audience will have an even more open mind to your content.

- So that people are more likely to follow your directions.

HOW THIS CAN BE ACHIEVED

- A well-written (but short!) bio demonstrating relevant experience/success.

- At presentations, an introduction by a respected host can use your bio and reinforce your "special powers" by adding personal comments.

- Having an EMA promoted by a respected third party.

- Evidence of past transformations through your own story and/or case studies.

- Presenting a proprietary model.

- Use of proprietary trademarks.

- Being a published author.

- Achieving best-selling book status.

- Use of proprietary terminology: e.g., "The Waterfall," "Black Jellybean."

- Use of stories, metaphors, analogies, and similes.

Note that while it is common practice to insert a bio at the rear of an e-guide or book, you're better to follow the practice of conference facilitators who read your bio *before* you speak.

That's because, in the old days when we only had physical books, it was relevant to have your bio on the rear cover, because people would read the title and then immediately flip the book over and check out the back cover.

But now that we've moved into the age of digital books, the back cover is not quite as easy to access as it used to be, and that's why you should have your bio right up in the front of your book or guide.

STEP FOUR: THE PROMISE

PURPOSE

- Motivates your Audience to pay attention and pre-sells them on your service.

OVERVIEW

- The Promise is a variation on your marketing message and Title and is often expressed as a statement that you need the Audience to believe in order for them to respond positively to your CTA. E.g., "to have control over your financial future, you can and you must develop lead-generation systems."

■ You can express this step as a "Core Message," and if you reference the subtitle Core Message in the Preface, you'll be able to refresh your memory, and in the process, you'll see a perfect example of what I'm writing about here.

WHY THIS IS IMPORTANT

■ Having alignment between the content of your EMAs and your service is important, because if someone has an interest in your EMA, they are more likely to be interested in your service as well.

■ By covertly embedding the benefit of your service into the start of your EMA in the form of a Core Message, you begin to shift a prospect's mind toward the idea that investing time and money in your service would be a wise decision.

HOW THIS CAN BE ACHIEVED

■ You can use your own story of transformation, illustrating your before and after experience. E.g., from broke to wealthy (wealth creation service), from fat to thin (weight loss service).

■ You can use before and after case studies in the form of client testimonials.

■ If you can't create client case studies because you are just starting out, then you can create avatars (e.g. Sam and Pam) and describe the typical before and after transformations a client would reasonably expect.

■ Often however, I'll state the Core Message in plain and simple terms, as I did in the Preface of this book, or by having the words of the message on one slide: e.g., in a webinar.

STEP FIVE: DESCRIBE THE PROBLEM AND SYMPTOMS OF NOT HAVING YOUR SERVICE

PURPOSE

- To motivate the Audience by having them feel their pain and their desire ("away from" and "toward" motivators) early in your EMA so they are primed to take action when you make your offer.

OVERVIEW

- This step creates a simple list of painful symptoms together with the emotion that each symptom evokes that will do the job.

WHY THIS IS IMPORTANT

- The motivation to buy starts with someone feeling an emotion.

- Painful emotions motivate more effectively in most people than desire-based emotions, but both can work depending on who your Ideal Client is. E.g., the more successful a business owner is the less likely they will be motivated by "away from" motivators.

- People will justify the purchase with a logical review of your service's features, including guarantees and case studies. However, this only becomes important *after* you've tap-danced on their subconscious and awakened memories that stimulate fear or desire-based emotions.

- When you accurately describe your Audience's problem and the symptoms they suffer from, you build massive Relatability.

HOW THIS CAN BE ACHIEVED

- Simply list or state between 3–5 symptoms (there is no magic number) and the emotions that go with them. E.g. *"you lose sleep worrying about where your next client is coming from"* or *"you feel disappointed that your efforts are not recognized by your boss"* or *"you sometimes experience frustration when someone who is an ideal client doesn't buy."*

- If your EMA is a presentation, then this step should not take more than two minutes. Books and guides (e-booklets) allow a bit more "real estate" and give you the opportunity to expand on each symptom, thereby helping the reader identify more fully with the stated symptoms.

- If it fits, then you can also use this step to point out that the definition of insanity would be to keep trying the same things but expect that these symptoms will go away.

STEP SIX: DESCRIBE WHAT THEY TRIED AND WHY IT DIDN'T WORK

PURPOSE

- To increase your credibility, believability, as well as relatability ("fly on the wall" experience and "oh, that's so true").

OVERVIEW

- This step lists your Audience's other options for solving their problem or meeting their need and removes all those options from their minds (the one option you leave them with is your service).

- You can label this step "common but costly mistakes" or similar.

WHY THIS IS IMPORTANT

- This is a very powerful psychological step that significantly enhances the likelihood that people will follow your recommendations, including your directions to accept the offer or respond to your CTA later in your EMA. E.g., at the end of your webinar, seminar, or special report.

- When you describe for the people what they already tried in respect to solving the problem, and why it didn't work, you drive Relatability to even deeper levels.

HOW THIS CAN BE ACHIEVED

- Cast your mind back to the mistakes you've made and all the mistakes that your clients have made over the years. What didn't work and why? The answer to those questions will give you the content for this step.

- In some instances, you can simply reverse the recommendations that you will make in the next step (where you present your Model) and give the mistake a fancy name: e.g., In my last book, I explained the benefit of scalability that EMAs provide, and the reverse (a common mistake) is the failure to develop EMAs.

- You can also cheat a little by searching the internet for content.

- Remember to use special titles where possible: e.g., "A failure to respect the principles of The Pipeline" or "Applying a High-Flow Strategy to a Low-Flow business."

- As mentioned, you can see how I did this, very explicitly, in Part Two of *Leadsology®: The Science of Being in Demand*, where I lay out 14 mistakes that most professionals make in attempting to generate demand, and indeed, again in this book in Part One and the section that features "Ten Traditionally Taught Marketing Methods To Avoid."

STEP SEVEN: INTRODUCE YOUR PROPRIETARY MODEL

PURPOSE

- Reveals how to make their pain disappear, and/or how their needs can be fulfilled.

- Also, further differentiates you from your competitors.

OVERVIEW

- Coco Chanel said, "in order to indispensable one must be different." If you have a proprietary model such as Leadsology,® you are suddenly "the only game in town."

- It's like you move from being one person in the middle of a continent surrounded by hundreds of competitors who all have their hand up and are shouting "pick me, pick me!" to being on your own island where you are the sole inhabitant and people must come to your island to get what they want.

WHY THIS IS IMPORTANT

- Eliminating direct competitors means more people want what you've got.

HOW THIS CAN BE ACHIEVED

- Break your service down into to a series of delivery steps, give each step a name or title, and create a draft model to give to a graphics expert to make it look nice and shiny.

- For an example, download my interactive model here: **www.leadsology.guru/the-model/** (note that your model does not have to be interactive).

Note that most people jump right into Step Seven at the start of their presentation, and in doing fail to build the Rapport, Respect, and Relatability they need in order for their Audience to have a receptive and open mind.

STEP EIGHT: EXPLAIN WHY THEY SHOULD NOT ATTEMPT TO IMPLEMENT ON THEIR OWN

PURPOSE

- To highlight the futility and stupidity of "do it yourself," and to eliminate DIY as an indirect competitor.

OVERVIEW

- I estimate that 95 percent of people who consume one of my EMAs and then decide to implement on their own will never do so.

- The remaining 5 percent who implement will fail to implement effectively because there are so many subtleties that they don't understand. In short, they simply don't have the skill or experience to implement effectively.

- The latter group are even worse off than the non-implementers, because they waste time and energy and wind up feeling frustrated and disappointed.

WHY THIS IS IMPORTANT

- It's our duty to tell people the truth about the consequences of self-implementation and the truth about the wisdom and efficacy of getting help from an experienced mentor, such as yourself.

- A failure to point out this "elephant in the room" does people a grave disservice and leads too many people to wrongly conclude the D.I.Y. is a viable option.

HOW THIS CAN BE ACHIEVED

- Create a story or a metaphor or a case study that explicitly illustrates the folly of DIY.

- Swipe and deploy the story I use from "Portuguese Irregular Verbs," where three men attempt to play tennis having only read a tennis rules book (buy the book if you want the full story).

- Or explain that DIY versus engaging a mentor is like the difference between removing your own ailing appendix and having a surgeon perform the operation.

- Or write/talk about how all the great sports stars in the world have a coach and continue to take lessons.

STEP NINE: MAKE YOUR CALL TO ACTION (CTA)

PURPOSE

■ Your CTA will often be to invite people to book a consult with you, but sometimes you may choose just to aim for new subscribers by giving your Audience a landing page where they can get another honey pot.

OVERVIEW

■ The best EMAs for getting consults booked are events such as webinars or seminars, and the latter is better than the former. However, they are a lot more work.

■ Books, and guides are better at growing your list than they are at having people buy directly, although new clients you get from a book will prove to be absolute premium quality because they are among the very few who are prepared to make a proactive effort at gaining new knowledge, and they tend to be a lot wealthier than people who simply download a short guide.

WHY THIS IS IMPORTANT

■ This is probably self-evident: You want a return on your investment of time, money, and energy either in the form of a sale or by growing your list.

HOW THIS CAN BE ACHIEVED

■ If your CTA is the offer of a consult so that attendees can talk with you about whether one of your services is a fit for their needs, then make sure you provide a means for them to easily book that meeting, ideally in the form of a dedicated URL: E.g. **www.bookachatwithtom.com** (go and grab your own URL right now) which automatically redirects to your scheduling platform.

STEP TEN: FOR BOOKS, GUIDES AND ONLINE MEETINGS – FREE RESOURCES SECTION

The primary purpose of books and e-books/guides is to grow your subscriber list.

The secondary purpose is to have readers make an inquiry about your services.

And a third purpose is to have your Audience buy something immediately, although most people who become clients will need a step in between reading your EMA and purchasing: e.g., attending an event or a consult.

Sadly, most people who buy your book or get your guide will not read them to the end!

You therefore need to offer free resources *right at the start* of your EMA.

Free resources will typically include online EMAs such as a diagnostic tool that shows a respondent the potential transformation when they engage your solution, an evergreen (automated) webinar training, a video series, access to interviews, a special report or a consult. The more the merrier!

The objective of offering these free resources (which are mini EMAs) is to capture the reader's contact details so you can nurture the relationship (BBB) with more EMAs until they are ready to buy.

Including a list of free resources at the very start of your EMA is *especially important for digital EMAs such as Kindle books or PDFs* because most people will open your EMA and give it a quick initial glance, but may never open it again.

So, by having a list of free resources right up front, you can capture their attention and get them to subscribe immediately, before your beautiful digital EMA is buried under an avalanche of other shiny things.

A SPECIAL NOTE ON THE USE OF FREE RESOURCES AT EVENTS

With most clients, I tend to recommend that they offer a free resource at the start of a webinar or seminar if they are going to be making an offer of a consult at the end of the event.

The reason is that, if you offer the free stuff at the end, some people will mistakenly decide to consume your free stuff and "see what it's like" before booking a time to talk with you. And of course, they'll then get distracted, go and chase someone else's shiny thing, and the opportunity is lost.

The Four Steps to Investment Validation

IT PROBABLY GOES without saying that when people are looking to work with you, they need to establish a level of confidence that they are making the right decision when investing with you.

But investment validation is a little bit like Audience segmentation in that there are different stages and segments, which, once we understand, give us the potential to make the buying decision a whole lot easier for our Audience.

The four investment validations are as follows:

VALIDATION #1: YOU

It may come as a surprise to you that most people who are looking to invest with you are initially far more concerned about your integrity than they are about the effectiveness of your service.

Another way of putting this is that you need to build Rapport and Respect as a bare minimum before most people will make the shift from checking you out to considering an investment in your services.

Putting this another way, many people care far more about whether you have integrity (definition: you walk the talk, you behave in a manner which is aligned with your stated values, you do what you say you are going to do) than they care about whether your service will deliver the results they want.

And that's why you should collect character-based testimonials as well as results-based testimonials. Neither one can take the place of the other.

You use these character-based testimonials on landing pages that you're directing fresh traffic to: e.g., from Other Peoples Networks or online advertisements, as opposed to landing pages that you're directing your own email subscriber list or social media followers to. That's because the people that already know you well won't need the character references.

Here's a few examples from one of my landing pages:

"Tom genuinely cares about your progress. He's generous with his time and resources, he listens, and draws on his deep experience and proven expertise to guide you forward."

Adam Gordon, Profit Leaks Detective

Profits Leak Detective

"Tom Poland is the real deal. No hype, no BS, what he says you'll get is what you get – or better. I trust him, and after 27 years in business, that trust is not given lightly."

This week ghostly

Leadership Engagement Specialist

"Tom is so much more than a master of marketing. He becomes a Mentor. But more than that, he becomes a friend, someone you can trust and rely on – he cares that much. And in case you didn't know that's what you needed, it becomes apparent to you very quickly. Tom's the real deal. I don't know how I'll ever repay him for his counsel."

Sean Quinlan, Attorney

You can see that none of the above mentioned the results that my clients enjoy; that comes with the next validation in step #2.

At this stage of my marketing, I simply want people to understand that I'm one of the good guys and not one of the hype and BS guys.

And just so I don't repeat myself here and bore you to bits, if you want more ways to have people validate your character, then pop back and read the Four Levels of Psychological Allure at the start of this part of the book.

VALIDATION #2: YOUR SERVICE

Unfortunately, there are a whole bunch of rip-off merchants out there in the marketplace and your Audience will have fallen victim to some of them prior to discovering the joyful potential of doing business with you.

This is especially true of the Explorers (see above) who outnumber those who will buy immediately by a factor of 4 to 1.

Explorers are cautious and careful, and they don't fall into the commonly accepted definition of a fool, who rushes in where angels fear to tread.

There are several tools at your disposal that will help your Audience validate that your service is a fit for their needs and that what you offer is effective.

These include testimonials and, most especially, from others in the same industry as your Audience. That's why on the Results page of my website at **www.leadsology.guru/results/** it's relatively easy to figure out the service that each client featured is offering.

And while we're on the subject of testimonials, and more specifically results-based testimonials, make sure that the testimonials you're collecting actually talk about specific results and not only character references.

At this stage of the investment validation steps, we need to move well beyond character-based testimonials, and so comments from your clients such as "I really like Sue and it's been a pleasure to work with her" are not going to cut the mustard.

You should also consign to the scrap heap any testimonials that talk excitedly about what might be possible in the future: e.g. "I'm really pumped about the future now that I've worked with John."

Ideally, what you want to do is collect testimonials that give a short and succinct summary of the before and after scenario that many in your Audience will be able to relate to. For example, this one from Derek Roberts, who serves busy, time-stressed executives in some of the world's largest food corporations:

"Whereas before it was difficult in the extreme to get the attention of my ideal clients, I now have a pipeline full of inquiries which have come in from the vice presidents of some of the world's largest corporations."

An even better way to allow prospects to validate that one of your services is a fit for their needs is to take the time and trouble to actually meet with them, ask them about the challenge/ problem they are facing, what they tried in the past, and how that worked (predictably, not very well, which is why they want to talk with you, but it helps you build Rapport, Respect, and Relatability) before moving on to discuss the features and benefits of your service that would be a best fit for meeting their needs.

In other words, offering a consult is a great way to allow your Audience to validate the fit between their needs and your service. I cover more on that concept in Multi-Directional Consults in Part Five.

I've run marketing sessions where I have fully explained in great detail how one of my programs works, including the fees, time commitment, the reformat, and whatever else you give a name to.

And following that type of session, I've had people sign up for the program that I was promoting (Seekers) and others who simply wanted to meet with me and confirm what they believed they already knew, which was that making the investment was the right thing to do (Explorers).

You can also offer a guarantee of satisfaction which preferably comes in the form of a money-back guarantee of which this is an example:

If you're not completely satisfied after having fully engaged with the Leadsology® Program over the first four weeks, simply email me directly before the start of the fifth week and you'll receive a full refund of any money paid. "Fully engaged" means that you will have completed the modules and action assignments and you will have attended the weekly Q&A session.

Lastly, you can use what I call Risk Reversal and let your Audience know that instead of them carrying the risk, you're prepared to carry it.

When I use this strategy, I explained to prospective clients that I don't want any money upfront. This can come as a shock to them but it's a terrific way to drive home that you're not like the hype and BS merchants.

I suggest that instead of them paying the upfront, that we work together for the first month and if they are not completely satisfied that they've made the right decision then they can walk away without paying a cent. No strings attached.

To be clear, I'm not offering to work with them for a full month for free, I'm simply saying that they can pay in arrears.

And if you're wavering about guarantees, ask yourself this: Why should someone who was almost a complete stranger trust you with their money, if you are not prepared to back yourself in regard to delivering more than full value?

Depending on the service I'm offering, I like to be able to say to prospective new clients, "don't trust me – instead, let me trust you," and then offer a Risk Reversal like the above.

VALIDATION #3: THEIR MONEY

Validation of their money is not just about a return on investment, although you can achieve that sort of validation very swiftly, both with the guarantees mentioned above, but also by figuring out exactly what would have to change in their business in order for them to have received a return on their investment with you.

For example, if I'm working with a consultant who invoices $50,000 on average, it's very easy for me to point out to them that one new client is going to more than cover my fees, and that if they walk away from our engagement with multiple streams of leads, then their investment with me will be one of the most profitable that they've ever made.

Risk Reversal combined with demonstrating the return on investment is one of the most effective ways to flip a person's mental switch from "maybe" to "definitely."

In addition to validating return on investment, some clients also need to validate affordability by looking at their monthly cash flow and seeing how much of that you're asking for.

For example, my current entry-level program runs over eight weeks and the investment is $2,000, but I also offer payment terms at the rate of $197 per month over 12 months.

That's correct: even though I deliver full value over an eight-week period, I will allow those who have cash flow constraints to pay me over a 12-month period.

It's a variation of the Risk Reversal strategy I mentioned above.

I've touched on the concept of people mistaking affordability with prioritization of expenditure, but it's also worth stating the bleeding obvious, which is that if you can make a thing more affordable for your Audience, then you get more sales.

Offering no deposit (as in the first Risk Reversal concept mentioned above), monthly payment options, and multiple price points for different levels of service are just some of the ways that you can be of more service to those on a more limited budget.

It's a little different if you don't have scalable value delivery embedded into your service, such as those offering an online course.

By contrast, if you're a consultant, it's quite appropriate, given that you effectively need to reinvent the wheel for each project, to charge premium prices, and that you don't feel the need to cater to those on a more limited budget.

To be even clearer: If you are offering bespoke services/advice, you should run quickly from anyone who wants to pay you over 12 months for a service that you deliver in say, two months.

Because there is another option which is to do what I do and offer the online group training program for a relatively low monthly investment, together with high-end, reassuringly expensive consulting services, along with a couple of options in between.

This appeals to a wider range of budgets and requirements, providing the opportunity each of them needs to validate their financial investment. And as you'll see shortly when I cover the subject of Multi-directional Consults, it generates more revenue as well.

VALIDATION #4: THEIR IMPLEMENTATION

Once again, this validation step is more for the Explorers than it is for the Seekers.

Some of your Audience will have bought programs or invested in services like yours previously but, unfortunately, haven't got a lot to show for it – and *not* because they bought something that was ineffective.

According to the surveys I've completed, a majority of people who don't gain full value for their investment in services, advice, or software, state that the reason had nothing to do with the supplier, but rather their failure to implement.

This is a very real and growing area of concern and it therefore needs to be addressed in a systematic and comprehensive manner.

Since I launched my first business development training program in 1995, I have been very mindful about creating structures which significantly increase the likelihood of implementation.

One of my clients, Frank, from Philadelphia, makes a feature of the fact that his team will hang around after they've completed a software development project to ensure that the end users of the software they've developed not only know how to use it but use it daily. It's a very significant feature, because without the end users using the software, there isn't much point in having invested in its development in the first place.

In most of my programs and services, I insist on a **weekly point of accountability and review** with every single client. Not fortnightly, because if for some reason they need to skip a meeting, then suddenly our meetings are one month apart and that means they can drift for too long in between our meetings.

In addition, you can lay out a series of **milestones** which let a prospective new client know exactly what they can expect to have achieved and when they will have achieved that during their engagement with you.

And to further demonstrate my willingness to support, every single client, regardless of the price point they select, gets my **mobile phone** number. Because most of my clients are in different time zones from me, I let them know that my phone will be off when I'm asleep, but that, nevertheless, they should feel free at any time to text or call me if they need help outside of the normal structure.

This is another surprise for prospective clients (a bit like Risk Reversal) which drives home the fact that I care, as another point of differentiation.

I've never had a client try to use this opportunity and it is rare that any of them even use it, mainly because the stand support structures are so effective. There is very little downside in me offering it.

You can also offer a **24/7 client-exclusive, online chat room** such as **www.slack.com**, a variation of which I use for all private mentoring clients so that we have a direct line of communication along with an easy-to-track thread of action items, instead of having communications buried in our respective avalanches of emails. Smartphone apps are also readily available for these type of online chat rooms, which adds an even higher level of service.

In addition, any time you take a complex process and break it down to a series of clear, highly prescriptive, **simple, step-by-step action items**, complete with relevant examples, templates, and case studies, then you dramatically increase the likelihood of clients implementing recommendations.

Lastly, if you want to increase implementation, then *don't* offer a comprehensive service.

Instead, make your value delivery as simple as possible by focusing on the 20 percent of what your clients need to do to achieve 80 percent of the potential result.

Your clients will be grateful, they'll implement more and, as a result, they'll gain more value than if you had insisted on a comprehensive treatment.

Additionally, if they really want to invest in the 80 percent that will give them the final 20 percent of the result, I'm sure that you'll be willing to send them invoices that are commensurately larger.

By way of a final thought, always bear in mind that if your clients fail to implement, they don't get value, and people who don't get value, don't refer other people to you.

It's therefore in everyone's best interest that you do whatever you reasonably can to create a structure that increases the likelihood of not just implementation, but correct implementation, by your clients.

Part Five:

MAXIMIZING YOUR CONVERSIONS

Maximizing Your Revenue Potential Through Multi-Directional Consults

FOR A LOT of people, the Holy Grail of marketing would be to set up an evergreen webinar that runs automatically on the hour every hour and offers a link at the end whereby people can purchase a program or course that's downloadable or consumable by the purchaser while the supplier is on holiday or asleep.

Personally, I don't know of anyone who has cracked that one. I know people who say they've cracked it, but their reputation is such that I'm inclined not to believe them, a belief which is probably validated by the fact that they appear to be working seven days a week still.

But even the idea, which I'll be the first to admit is very appealing, may not be all that it's cracked up to be.

That's because as human beings we are wired to experience deeper and more enduring levels of happiness and fulfillment, when we are being of helpful service to others.

I'm very clear in my advice to those who want to grow their business so that one day they can sell it and do "what I *really* want to do."

The fastest route to true happiness is to decide that you want to do what you do, because you enjoy doing it.

It's really only a mental switch that you need to flip, an attitude change, to take the short step from the stress of working because you want something else, to working because it is what you want to do and because you find it fulfilling.

I appreciate that the idea of bringing some passion to what we do is not a new one; it's probably thousands of years old and certainly I wrote about it extensively in my first book in 2005 entitled *Your Extraordinary Life*. I had taught professionally on the same subject for 20 years prior.

But the concept of achieving happiness and fulfillment through our work is relevant to the proposed Holy Grail mentioned above, because even if it were possible to achieve endless flows of money while we do practically nothing, there would be an emptiness about it that would inevitably result in a discontinuance of the practice.

Unfortunately, my Internet search skills have failed me and I've been unable to find a survey that I've previously read about, where respondents were asked a question along the lines of the following:

"If you could take a pill and make all your problems and challenges disappear and stay in a state of perpetual bliss, would you swallow the pill? Or would you prefer to live life in all its harsh realities?"

Surprisingly, to me at least, a large majority of respondents said they would refuse to take such a pill.

As the late great Yogi Berra said, *"if the world was a perfect place, it wouldn't be."*

If you accept that the key to fulfilling your Life Purpose is to be found in serving more people, more effectively, then you'll like what I am about to suggest.

The Multi-directional Consult is a term I created to describe a method for that achieves the following:

#1. Converting more leads into clients.

#2. Increasing your revenue without expending any more time.

#3. Being of service to more people.

#4. Being of more effective service to more people.

#5. Avoid on-boarding the wrong type of client.

When the Roman Empire was at its peak, it was said that all roads led to Rome.

For most of my clients, all Leadsology LeadStreams® lead to a consult.

Pretty much every reader will be aware that the idea of a consult is to determine whether a prospect has a problem/challenge/opportunity that you can help with.

Despite what the sales conversion trainers will tell you, the purpose of the consult is not, I repeat not, to convert *every* prospect into a client, but rather only the ones that are a fit for what you have to offer.

In Part Four, I mentioned the truism that, when all you have is a hammer, everything looks like a nail.

Equally true is that when you only have one level of service and one price point, it's very tempting to recommend that solution at that price point, to every prospect.

But if you have 3-5 options for each prospect then you're more likely to recommend something that represents more of a customized solution to that person's needs and budget.

In the past, I have sold programs by inserting a website address leading to a sales page, or by promoting that same website address at the end of the webinar, conference presentation, and so on.

But these days I prefer to offer prospects what I call a Multi-directional Consult, whereby we meet and discuss their needs and what they have tried in the past to solve their marketing challenges, how that worked, and then to see which, if any, of the solutions that I could offer would be a fit for their needs and budget.

This way, I can make the most appropriate recommendation, which could be a $197 group coaching program, a small mastermind-style coaching program for $12,000, a private "done with you" option for $25,000, a "done for you" end to end Leadsology LeadStreams® system for $100,000, or indeed, referring that person to something or someone else who would be a closer fit to their needs.

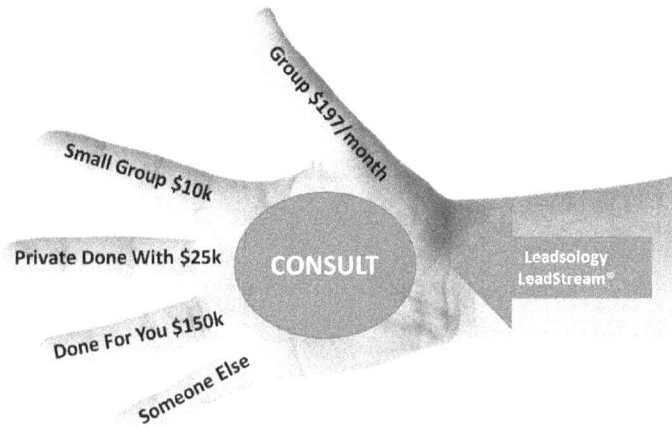

I was speaking with a corporate training and consultant client, Mark from Sydney, Australia, about his average transaction size for his corporate training programs, which at that stage was something like $12,500.

I recommended that he create a $50,000 package.

"Why on earth what I want to do that?" he asked.

"Well," I responded, "how many $50,000 packages will you sell if you don't have one?"

"Um, not too many?" he quite rightly guessed.

"Mark," I said, "flipping this around, I will bet you dollars to donuts, that once a year you will have a new client that will buy the most expensive thing that you have to offer."

On a similar note, I'll never forget the day that I submitted a proposal to help the software developer, Sam from London, UK, to embed lead-generation systems into his business.

It was a $25,000 deal, which for me at the time represented a very big deal.

When we had a follow-up meeting to find out if he wanted to go ahead, I discovered that he hadn't even opened the proposal. So, with WebCams on at both ends, he found my email and opened the proposal.

So, there was me, trying to appear relaxed, but on the inside feeling quite tense, awaiting his reaction.

He read the proposal, mumbling as he went through it. After a minute or two, he got to the bottom line, literally, and figuratively.

His eyes widened, and his jaw dropped a little.

I thought I was a goner.

But to my surprise, his reaction was not because he thought my fee was too high, but rather that it was very low.

"Wow", he said, "that's great, last year I hired a marketing consultant and paid him $150,000 and really, all I've got left to show for it is a good-looking website but it doesn't even capture the contact details of visitors."

Naturally I was initially delighted that he had accepted my proposal, but then a little later I was feeling rueful when I realized that I'd probably left a good $125,000 "on the table" with that deal.

The good news is that Sam hired me twice, so I was able to make up some of the shortfall over the following 12 months.

Multi-directional Consults are a terrific alternative to the standard one-direction Consult or trying to sell by embedding a buying link in one of your Assets, because they allow you to help more people, more effectively while at the same time increasing your revenue.

How to Increase the Quality of Inquiries With Auto-Filters

When you set up multiple Leadsology LeadStreams® in your business and begin to enjoy a flow of inbound new client inquiries every week, you move from a poor-quality problem to a high-quality problem.

The poor-quality problem that you previously experienced was not enough new client inquiries.

The high-quality problem is that you may now suffer from is too many inquiries and you will need a way to filter out those who are unlikely to be a fit for your services.

It's worthwhile bearing in mind that when you make it easier for people to book a consult, they will be of lower quality, in respect to the likelihood that the prospects will fit with your service and their ability to afford you.

But there are bunch of ways that you can improve the quality of the people you meet with and here are a few to get you started.

Note that all the methods described below finish with the prospect landing on a webpage where they can select and book a time to speak with you. Find yourself an online scheduling platform for this purpose.

FILTER #1. Direct interested people to a landing page that describes the purpose of the consult (that it's to talk about working together) and what it's not (a free coaching session or a sales ambush). Make sure they understand the minimum fees involved if they work with you, and state very clearly the type of people you work with and those who you don't work with. At the end of the page, they must click a little box to indicate that they fully read and fully understand the terms and conditions of booking the Consult.

FILTER #2. In some marketplaces, the above filter is enough. If you find it's not enough however, then you add a second page that those who have completed the above page are then taken to. If you include the second page, then at some point on the first page you need to explain to your prospect what's going to happen. Filter #2 is a webpage where your prospect is asked to complete a series of questions about their business, including current revenue, full-time equivalent number of employees, and whatever else might be relevant, It also serves the purpose of having them jump through some digital hoops as a way of validating how serious they are.

FILTER #3. The most robust filtering process includes the above but adds another page, just prior to the online scheduling page, that asks them to pull out their credit card and pay for the consult. Again, if you include this filter, this should be explained as part of the process on the very first landing page in Filter #1.

I have a webpage that I don't promote publicly, but that is available when I want to refer people to it. It explains that I charge $1,000 an hour for one-off consulting work. I then provide them with a coupon code which will reduce that fee to $100 as a special, limited-time offer.

This means that they can place a value on meeting with me and at the same time make them feel like they're getting a very good deal, which they are.

After years of playing with various filters, there is no doubt that incorporating all the above three filters works best for my market.

However, I would not recommend those filters for anyone with a corporate Audience.

That's because executives are amongst the most time-poor and stressed individuals on the planet.

And charging a fee for an initial consult means nothing to them, because their company would pay for it and it only places an unnecessary obstacle in their way.

Any busy executive who is prepared to sacrifice a part of their day to talk with you about the potential of hiring you has demonstrated enough serious intent simply by being prepared to sacrifice some of the time.

Use consult filters to strike a balance between the quantity and quality of consults that works well for you.

PART SIX

LEVERAGING YOUR RESULTS
THROUGH SCALABILITY

Scaling Results Through OPT

OPT **STANDS FOR** Other People's Time.

Until you learn to get results through OPT, you'll never get both the lifestyle and the results you truly desire.

Every Leadsology® LeadStream® that I create and that my clients have embedded into their businesses is painstakingly put together during a process of continual testing, observing, and refining.

The result is a lead-generation stream that can be put into place one small step at a time. This means that what might otherwise have been a relatively complex system can be simpler to implement, because the client only needs to action one step at a time.

But there's a very significant additional benefit when a complex lead-generation system is broken down into a series of simple steps.

To illustrate the point, allow me to reintroduce you to one of the most remarkable business minds of the 20th century, Mr. Henry Ford, who as everyone knows initiated a global revolution in vehicle manufacturing.

At one stage, Henry Ford was producing 30 cars per employee, per year, while his nearest rival at Packard was producing 2.67 cars per man, per year.

Not only was productivity at the Ford motor plant some 10 times greater than it was at the plant of his closest competitor, Henry Ford also paid his workers five dollars a day which was double what was paid at Packard.

And lest you are in danger of thinking that Ford was pumping out poorer quality vehicles, nothing could have been further from the truth. Ford vehicles were far more robust and much less subject to breakdown then those of his competitors, even compared to more expensive vehicles at the luxury end of the market.

There is a lot that Henry Ford did to achieve his remarkable accomplishments.

But at the heart of it all was his ability to break down a complex manufacturing process, that of producing an automobile, into a series of simple steps.

Ford identified 7,822 "motions," or segments as I like to call them, that formed a sequence of actions that accumulated in the efficient production of a high-quality motor vehicle.

Similarly, by identifying each step/segment in a Leadsology LeadStream® that results in the generation of inbound new client inquiries, I like to think that I've released the potential for both greater quality and a higher numbers of leads.

Take for example the Leadsology LeadStream® that I call Boardroom Briefings.

In one of our earlier versions, I segmented the process and listed each step as follows:

1. Daily LinkedIn connection request

2. Monitor connection request

3. Responder personalized responses

4. Invite to register

5. Send invitation message

6. Responder personalized responses

7. Attendee registers online

8. Attendee receives meeting-linked email

9. Email/SMS reminders go out to registrants

10. Briefing is conducted

11. Attendee books Consult time

12. Attendee receives consult-meeting email link

13. Email/SMS reminders sent to prospect

14. Consult conducted

15. Follow-up created

When you create a segmented list of actions you then get the opportunity to scale your results by asking two questions of every item, which are:

Question one: Can I automate this?

Question two: Can I outsource this?

I determined that I could automate items 1, 7, 8, 9, 11, 12 and 13 in the above list.

It's not within the scope of this book to explain exactly how I can achieve that, but by way of example, we can set up email/SMS reminders inside the online scheduling platform that we use for both Boardroom Briefings and Consults, thus automating that particular segment.

I also figured out that I could outsource items 2, 4, 5 and 15.

That left me with items 3, 6 and 14, and I subsequently figured out how to outsource item 3, which left me only with the Boardroom Briefing and the Consult to conduct, both of which are highly profitable and which I also happen to enjoy.

The following is an example of a happy marriage of inclination and profitability.

OLOGY

Enjoy A Weekly Flow of Inbound, New Client Inquiries

Leadstreams™

ASSET: Boardroom Briefing   **AUDIENCE:** LinkedIn   **CODE:** BBLI

Phase 2: Execution

	Step	Automated	Outsource	Insource	Swipe	System
1	Daily connection requests	✓			Swipe	System
2	Monitor connection requests		✓		Swipe	System
3	Respond to personalized responses			✓	Swipe	System
4	Invite to opt-in		✓		Swipe	System
5	Send invitation message		✓		Swipe	System
6	Respond to personalized responses			✓	Swipe	System
7	Attendee registers online	✓			Swipe	System
8	Attendee receives meeting link email	✓			Swipe	System
9	Email/SMS reminders to attendees	✓			Swipe	System
10	Briefing conducted	✓		✓	Swipe	System
11	Attendee book Consult time	✓			Swipe	System
12	Attendee receives meet link email	✓			Swipe	System
13	Email/SMS reminders to attendees	✓			Swipe	System
14	Consult conducted			✓	Swipe	System
15	Follow up created		✓		Swipe	System

Not only can I outsource the process of making 50 daily connection requests, for as little as $60 a month, but I also shed the aspects that I would never have persisted in, they being monotonous processes I would have avoided because I got "a better offer" to do something more interesting with my time.

In automating that segment, I've replaced hours of tedious and un-enjoyable work with work that I enjoy, and that's a whole lot more profitable and profitable, such as conducting consults. You would think that the option of automating or outsourcing where possible would be something of a no-brainer. But when I look around me, it appears that the majority don't agree with me, because so many are still stuck in unnecessary day-to-day drudgery. Or, simply not doing any consistent, persistent marketing.

Automating and outsourcing increases efficiency and effectiveness while reducing expenses, conserving my time, and eliminating drudgery from my life. Even more importantly, the things that need to get done, get done.

In addition, the contractors who work on the Leadsology® team enjoy the work and are relatively well-paid. It's a win-win for everyone.

Another way of looking at this is to think of yourself as an orchestra conductor.

As the orchestra conductor, I have one person in charge of each part of the Leadsology LeadStreams® orchestra. That contractor is responsible for, and is remunerated for, both the quality and quantity of leads flowing from the stream they direct and/or oversee.

Each contractor receives training and is supported by a series of step-by-step systems, with coaching at weekly meetings. Targets are agreed to, results are tracked and measured, and every system is an open book for the contractor so that, wherever possible, they can see the results of their efforts 24/7.

As such, each contractor is truly empowered to achieve and be rewarded at the highest possible level.

It's like I have a lead violinist, a lead cellist, and so on, one in charge of each section of the Leadsology LeadStreams® orchestra.

To summarize the benefits of segmentation and orchestra conducting consider these points:

1. You free up enormous amounts of your own time.

2. You increase revenue and profitability exponentially.

3. You spend more of your time doing the things you prefer to do.

4. You spend more of your time doing the things that you're damned good at.

5. You provide income to families that might otherwise struggle in countries where secure and well-paid employment is difficult to find.

6. You enjoy more consistency and reliability in your lead generation because you have a team of people who are motivated and equipped to generate the results you want, on your behalf.

SCALING RESULTS THROUGH OBSERVATION

In a study reported in the February 26 issue of *Nature* (Vol. 391, pp. 871-874), researchers at the Weizmann Institute of Science conducted a highly controlled experiment demonstrating how a beam of electrons was affected by the act of being observed.

I am the last one who would want to get into the technical scientific details of this phenomena, but there is also a commercial equivalent reported in the book *In Search of Excellence* authored by Peters and Waterman in 1982.

(Yes, I'm old enough to remember that.)

What the authors found is that, when a group of factory workers realized that the level of their productivity was being measured, productivity increased.

What they also reported is that the productivity didn't have to be measured; rather, it was enough to simply tell people that the productivity was going to be measured.

And so, it's clear both from the world of quantum mechanics as well as the world of business, that observation has the potential for significant impact on our results.

The greatest single marketing capability that any of us can possess is the simple act of accepting responsibility for the observation of results, as well as the trialing of new initiatives.

That said, each of us can measure and observe the results of whatever lead-generation efforts we're currently employing.

Naturally, it's important to provide team members, be they employees or contractors, with both numerical and subjective feedback, the latter being your opinion on how they are doing in response to both their feedback and results.

But the challenge is that, once you've got multiple Leadsology LeadStreams® set up, there's a whole lot of data that you need to observe.

To make the collection of marketing data easier and simpler to collect as well as timelier and more accurate, I created a lead-generation dashboard, using a very sophisticated Microsoft Excel spreadsheet, which allows for both the identification of lead generation KPIs (Key Performance Indicators) as well as tracking the same.

I've also set up a webpage where you can download a free version of the dashboard so that you can create your own lead-generation dashboard.

Here's the link: **www.leadsology.guru/dashboard/**

When you go to that webpage, you will find a video and instructions on how to use the dashboard to greatest effect.

A word to the wise: most entrepreneurs don't wake up in the morning thinking "Yippee! Today is the day I get to fill out a spreadsheet!"

The reason I mention this is that, personally, I have my wonderful operations manager, Olivia, who resides in the Philippines, update our dashboard so I don't have to take headache pills every day.

You might like to consider doing the same.

PART SEVEN:

LEADSOLOGY® RESULTS

THE FOLLOWING ARE comments from clients who have graduated from one of Tom Poland's programs, which are embedded with the principles, strategies, and structure of Leadsology.® These results are from clients who "imperfectly persisted" in implementing the strategies from his program. Results like these are not achieved by all clients and results are dependent on many factors external to Tom Poland's control.

My market is CEOs and VPs of global food corporations. In the past, getting my message noticed by such senior people was difficult in the extreme.

But thanks to Leadsology® LeadStreams®, I now have a full pipeline of new client inquiries from Directors and C-Suite Execs of some of the world's biggest food corporations including Coke, Mars, and Unilever. To be honest, I'd never have thought this sort of result was possible and I'm relieved and delighted.

Derek Roberts, Consultant

✳ ✳ ✳

Prior to Leadsology® I was generating six figures, but almost killing myself scrambling around for clients.

I'm now having more fun, generating five times the number of new clients and in less time than I ever thought possible.

Christina Force, Coach and Trainer

✳ ✳ ✳

When we started working with Tom Poland we already had one or two marketing systems in place, but we weren't getting any results.

Then we applied the Leadsology® LeadStreams® methodology and whereas before we had frequent gaps in our bookings, now we're often booked out weeks ahead.

Gordon Dickson. Kinesiologist

During the first twelve months that I worked with Tom Poland our **revenue increased by 43% to over $1,000,000 and my net personal earning's rose by 50 % to $400,000.**
We achieved the goals with no sacrifice of personal leisure time and we continue to enjoy an "earnings per partner hour" which is amongst the top quartile in the country.

Steve Bennet, Bennet and Associates

Before working with Tom Poland's program I was very clear about where I want to take the business to, but I had no idea of how to get there and I thought, "If I work any harder I'll kill myself." **But while I was working with Tom our turnover exploded, we more than quadrupled our revenue and profits increased by over 300%.** *At the same time I worked a lot less. My investment with Tom has paid off more than tenfold. Tom's program certainly delivers on its promises.*

Ginny Scott, M.D. Capulet

In the first year of working with Tom my earnings increased by just over 100%.
One of the biggest benefits was discovering how to strengthen my ability to systematically attract very high quality new clients into my practice. In addition I was able to set realistic but challenging goals in my business and personal life to achieve a more realistic work life balance.

Greg Moyle. Managing Director, NZFP

The corporate business environment we work in is very complex. Our ideal clients are senior executive and C-level people for whom business is a matter of high stakes, and they are therefore slow to trust and very discerning when selecting new consultants. Tom Poland's Leadsology Program has enabled me to not only find the right leads, but to build a relationship of trust and rapport with them to the point where they have gone from barely knowing about us, to trusting us with their most critical M&A Acquisitions. As a result, I enjoy a lead pipeline that is continually full of high-quality, inbound, new client, inquiries.

Thomas Kessler, Consultant

❖ ❖ ❖

Prior to joining Tom Poland's program I was working 60 – 70 hours a week and I had only one afternoon off work on the weekends. Now a typical work week for me is about three days. **Our profit has tripled and so I'm making a lot more money out of what I'm doing.**

Tom's program is priceless. I couldn't put a price on where the program has taken me from and where I am now.

Dianne Bussey, FACT Solutions Consulting

Anything that doubles your income has got to be good and that's exactly what happened while working with Tom Poland.

I gained an additional depth to my personal life and business life. I've got more leisure time, I have more holidays, and I earn more. I recommend Tom Poland to anyone in charge of a business.

Geoff Wilson, Professional Consulting Group

❋ ❋ ❋

Before working with Tom Poland's program my business was "all me". I was working insane hours and I thought there had to be a better way.

Now I've freed up a lot of time including 12 weeks holiday a year as well as **growing the business by over 400% and adding several million dollars to turnover and the bottom line of my business.**

Fred Soar, Soar Printing

I started working with Tom Poland 18 months ago and already I've doubled my earnings

I now also enjoy three months holidays every year whereas for the last 31 years I've worked almost seven days a week.

I've experienced dramatic changes in both my business and personal life.

John Good, Good Financial Services

Before joining Tom Poland's program around 2000 I was working 60 – 70 hours a week. Once we started working together I grew my number of employees from six to over 30 and **I sold one of my businesses for many millions thanks in no small part to working with Tom's program.**

I've spent a week with Richard Branson on his private island and dined personally with Google founder Larry Page thanks to Tom challenging me to think bigger and to follow my passion. And I'm pleased to still be working with Tom some eight years later. Joining Tom's program was certainly one of the best business decisions I've ever made.

Mark Rocket, Rocket Lab, Avatar and others

❖ ❖ ❖

Before joining Tom Poland's program I'd reached a point where I couldn't see how I was going to grow the business more because I was drowning in detail. Now my time is freed up to think more clearly and more creatively. **We've gone from being static to buying out a competitor because we've boosted our profits significantly.**

And time off was always an issue for me but now I take at least one week off every quarter and three weeks at Christmas and I feel good about that. If you are prepared to make changes the value of Tom Poland's program is massive.

Ian Telford, Jason Products

As a result of working with Tom Poland the value of my business increased by many millions of dollars.

Before joining Tom's program I was working six and seven days a week. Now I achieve more and yet I only work four days a week.

My advice for any business owner who wants to enjoy more revenue and a better quality lifestyle, is to get on with it by joining Tom Poland's program.

Grant Faber, Superbrokers Logistics Ltd

In the last 12 months since I started working with Tom Poland my earnings have more than doubled and I'm ahead of my target again this year.

I've gone from having 4 weeks holiday per year to 13 weeks. I've quit smoking, lost 4 kilograms of weight and I'm fitter than I've ever been before.

I credit these achievements to my commitment to working with Tom Poland.

If you own a business then it's likely that working with Tom will be the best investment you'll ever make.

Warren Storm, Storm Financial, Life Brokers NZ Ltd

Prior to working with Tom Poland's program I was running a reasonably successful business but since then **sales have increased and profits have increased quite considerably.**

But the success at work has been balanced by ongoing success at home and with my health as well and that's been important to me.

Tom's programs may appear to be pricey but it's also a question of value because in my case, I've recovered the cost of his program many times over.

Alan Coop, Intercad Ltd

❖ ❖ ❖

After joining Tom Poland's program **within nine months I've boosted profits and generated more revenue than the last three years put together.**

The actual overall improvement as a complete package in my business has been substantial and that's allowed me to become semi-retired.

Gilbert Chapman, Debt Recovery Group

❖ ❖ ❖

Prior to working with Tom Poland I was working long and hard but the business wasn't growing and I felt frustrated about that.

Thanks to working with Tom my business rapidly increased in value and is now worth millions.

I can think of no reason why anyone who wants to add six or seven figures to their revenue would not apply to join Tom's program.

My investment has paid off a thousand fold. Tom's program worked with me and I know of others who have had a similar result.

Win Charlebois, The Diamond Shop

Bonus Chapter:

Essential Infrastructure Assets For Effective Marketing Systems

THE FOLLOWING PLATFORMS are for use and recommend in Leadsology LeadStreams® to automate and systematize as many individual steps/segments as possible.

Some links may contain affiliate cookies and so, if you just hate the idea of me making a little money in helping you, then don't click the link!

For our email database and marketing platform we use **www.infusionsoft.com**

To register people for online events or consults we use **www.scheduleonce.com**

To automate connection requests and messaging in LinkedIn we use **www.linkedprospect.com**

To automate emailing all manner of OPN prospects we use **www. mailshake.com**

To conduct online events and consults we use:
www.gotomeeting.com and **www.zoom.us**

For those starting out with email platforms we recommend **www.mailer-lite.com**

For our image library we use **www.123rf.com**

For video recording and production, we use Camtasia from **www.techsmith.com**

www.ingramcontent.com/pod-product-compliance
Lightning Source LLC
Chambersburg PA
CBHW061135220326
41599CB00025B/4238